UNDERSTAND CHILD DEVELOPMENT

So You Don't Have to Say,
"I Wish I Had Known That!"

A. Lynn Scoresby, Ph.D.
Alvin Price, Ph.D.

UNDERSTAND CHILD DEVELOPMENT

*"So You Don't Have To Say
"I Wish I Had Known That!"*

A. Lynn Scoresby, Ph.D.
Alvin Price, Ph.D.

Knowledge Gain Publications
703 South State Street, Suite One
Orem, Utah 84058
(801) 225-9588
Fax (801) 225-9498
http://www.familyadv.com

Grateful acknowledgment is made to Ashley Hibdon, Anneka Scoresby, and Nancy Heaton De Loach for editing this book and to Dan Scoresby for cover design.

© 1998 Knowledge Gain Publications
Orem, Utah

Printed in the United States of America
ISBN
1-884518-50-8

Table of Contents

Concepts of Child Development

Behavioral scientists have studied many aspects of human behavior. This concentrated effort by thousands of researchers and writers has yielded much useful and significant information about human development. In spite of all that has been done, there is one condition or variable that has not been well-researched: the factor of time and how it influences what we are.

In a general way, of course, we have some theories that suggest that events early in life influence what happens later. But for the most part, we still have difficulty trying to understand how time becomes an influential part of the human personality.

The matter of time is of increased importance when we focus on human development. Development takes place over time, and scientists suggest that it is orderly instead of random and confused. Further, development appears to have a direction of some sort, which means it has a goal or objective. Some believe that development is continuous and others suggest that it is sporadic. Regardless of which position you accept, none of these ideas are useful if one does not see and understand them in relation to time.

As a practical matter, we are interested in what happens to a child of any age during certain segments of time. We want to know what happens, what causes it to happen, and what might influence it. Why? For one thing, we are interested in these questions from a scientific point of view. Development is significant and studying about it may improve the human condition. Development sometimes is not successful. It can be adversely affected by many things. For those who guide children including parents, teachers, physicians, and church leaders, knowledge about ineffective development is essential.

Imagine observing a child and noticing something interesting or unusual about him. Let's suppose you notice your four year old playing and having fun in the living room of your house. Then, you put on his coat and put him in the car to run a few errands. To your surprise, instead of being pleasant, he begins to whine, say mean words, and tease his little sister. From your point of view, you are annoyed with what he is doing. Should you spank him, yell at him, or ignore what is happening? What you do will depend on how you interpret this event. Is it just the changeability one expects from a four year old? Is it that the child does not like cars? Is he a big tease and likes to torment? Or, is it a manifestation of something that is developmental?

If you are unaware of the behavior being developmental, you might spank or scold. Before the age of three, children do not have a concept of rules. Over time they begin to think rules are part of every situation. Four-year-old children are very interested in rules, and when they do not know them, they will misbehave in order to find out. Knowing this developmental information, you will neither spank nor scold. You will take the time to teach your children the rules for specific situations. You may also have a good time doing it and then all you will need to do is remind them.

The Human Design

Probably the best way to understand development over time is to understand that humans have built-in or inherited mechanisms for both time and development. Inside the brain we can find a small mechanism that moves much like a clock. It actually rocks and keeps pace with time. New development takes place after certain amounts of time have passed and been measured by the brain's mechanism. In addition, microbiologists have found "master" genes on some chromosomes which control the expression of other genes. These lie dormant until a certain amount of time has passed and then act to signal other genes which influence further development.

In addition to these built-in features of brain and body, other conditions exist which stimulate and manifest development. All infants, for example, demonstrate an orienting response which allows them to move or orient their body in order to take full advantage of the world around them. This has the net effect of adding stimulation which promotes their development. Every infant also demonstrates an inherited "competency motivation," or drive, to improve physical and mental skills. This motivation is evidenced by children's motivation to turn over, crawl, walk, and run. It is manifest by children's motivation to learn language and acquire new mental skills.

Enlargement and Integration

Generally, as time passes and development takes place, an individual's capacity for thoughts, feelings, and skills is enlarged. One who is more mature thinks more advanced thoughts, feels more refined emotions, and can do more complex skills than the one who is less mature. Knowing this, you can expect yourself and your children to think more effectively and develop emotionally as you and they grow.

While this enlargement gradually appears, another form of development is also happening. It is called integration. This means that as the brain matures, it increases its capacity to collect information and integrate it into increasingly complex under-standings. Young children could tell one person apart from others and could tell that individuals belong to families. It would take more mature children to under-stand that families are part of towns which are part of cities, counties, states, countries, worlds, and solar systems. It would take a fairly integrated mind to know the various ways all these parts may be related or connected to one another.

What does this mean to you? If you understand that humans develop over time, then you will have an enlarged capacity for understanding children and yourself. Further, you will see your ideas about chil-dren become more integrated and your treatment of them will come closer to their situation in time. Collectively, if we all improve our understanding of development, we can improve our abilities to rear children until they become humane, responsible, and mature adults. ❀

Theories of Child Development

Years ago, doctors were attempting to learn how diseases spread. Not knowing about bacteria, they developed a theory based on what they thought they knew from what they observed. Imagine what preventive strategies they arrived at when they first thought that infections were spread by the wind. Their advice was to keep children from drafts and ill people away from fresh air. After discovering the idea of contagion by air, they thought perhaps the cause was the smell of illness. They supported this idea with the belief that when ill people in hospitals were separated from one another, meaning they could not smell sickness; there was less transmission of disease.

Bacteria in the role of infection was discovered in a hospital where doctors realized they were spreading it by using unsterilized surgical instruments. The first people operated on did not get the same illnesses as those who had later operations. Someone noticed this, realized it must be due to something going on in the operating room, and suspected the cause of infectious disease was something they could not see. Later, with the development of the microscope, the existence of bacteria was confirmed.

Researchers studying child development and human behavior started out with ideas as strange as the thought that smell causes disease. These early ideas were useful, though, because they could be disproved. This led to progressively better ideas until our present time. We now know that we do not know everything. There may be new and exciting discoveries made about children, and we should be open to learning about them. However, for you who are new to the study of child development, it is important to learn what has been thought about children so that you can use these ideas to generate or understand new discoveries.

Theories Are the Beginning

Everyone uses theories. You may have some ideas about how to get a date, the best way to buy a car, how to make friends, or how to get money from your parents. Such theories are part of everyday life and are so common you probably give them little thought. Your theories will be good or bad depending on whether they work the way you hope. When they work (i.e., you get a date), you conclude your theory is a good one. When desired results are not obtained (i.e., you cannot make friends), you will revise your theory by first questioning what went wrong, getting some new information, and then trying again.

This same process is an ongoing effort in the study of human behavior. Researchers try things out. If they seem to work, the theory seems to be a good one; if they fail, the theory is revised.

In our case, we are especially interested in those theories which are used to explain child development. As you begin your study, you should understand what a theory is. A theory is an organized and focused set of ideas. Since humans are so complex, a theory narrows what we are able to observe. One theory, for example, might focus on observable external behavior while another might focus our attention on inward thoughts or feelings.

(1) Theories have original, or "a priori," assumptions, which are the beginning or originating ideas for the theory. (2) A theory describes a "behavioral domain." This is usually found in a set of terms or vocabularies which explain what one sees when child behavior is observed. The word "maturation" refers to growth determined by biological factors, while "learning" refers to growth determined by children's experience with the environment. (3) Besides a vocabulary that identifies a behavioral domain, a theory also

contains predictions which are used to speculate what causes growth and what can be expected in the future. For instance, we can predict that all human beings will mature and go through puberty, a time of rapid biological growth. (4) Theories are not a set of wild ideas. Theories are partially proven systems of thought which are supported by much research but still contain some unproven ideas called "hypotheses." These hypotheses are the exciting parts of theories because they are at the forefront of knowledge, where scientists are working to confirm or disprove how children develop. Each theory proposes methods of proving or disproving hypotheses.

Four Theories

When you study a theory, it is important for you to learn about its assumptions. Then you can tell where it started and how researchers and writers have developed the theory over the years. In addition, you can find out what part of human behavior the theory is going to focus on and what part it is not. Consider the following.

Behavior Theories

Behavior theories begin with the assumption that humans inherit some survival drives such as hunger, thirst, sex, and perhaps curiosity. When individuals seek to satisfy these drives to survive, they learn. This learning is based on two laws: the law of association and the law of effect. When we attempt to satisfy our hunger, we learn all we can about what is associated with food and our bodily response to food. This is the law of association. We also learn what will get us food (i.e., money). Thus, we will learn what we must do to get money in order to get food. This is the law of effect.

Behavior theories focus on external behavior. They contain words which direct us to understand a stimulus and response, to count the frequency of some act, or to learn how some action may be reinforced or extinguished. In addition, they try to explain what external actions are related or associated with certain emotions.

Psychoanalytic Theories

Psychoanalytic theories begin with the assumption that humans inherit certain mental and emotional characteristics. These inherited tendencies develop in a sequence of age stages. This means that at certain ages, children will manifest certain mental and emotional characteristics. A second assumption is that the rate of development can be affected by the nature of one's exposure to the environment. That is, any new thoughts or feelings are largely affected or determined by the type of experience in our past. For example, if our parents were mean to us, we might be afraid and later assume that all people will hurt us. As time passes and we collect our life experiences, all development is due to the "interaction" of inherited characteristics and these experiences.

Psychoanalytic theories focus on emotions and thoughts. The words of these theories describe the inward part of human behavior and consider systems of thought and feeling to be the most important parts of development.

Cognitive Theories

These theories begin with the assumption that humans inherit a brain structure which determines certain styles of thought or cognition. It is proposed, for example, that cognitive development takes place in some age stages and is affected by how rich or limited one's interaction is with the environment. The richer our exposure, the better and more elaborate will be our ability to think and reason.

Cognitive theories describe several different mental activities, or "cognitive operations," and are used to explain or predict what will happen at certain stages of growth and what will help or hurt development (e.g., neglecting children will hinder development while much positive exposure to people and things will help children grow).

Ethological Theories

Ethological theories are different from any of the other three types of theories. These theories start with the assumption that human development stems from inherited characteristics. Further, ethological theories focus on the behaviors which one exhibits toward other members of its species. These include eating, mating, survival, parenting, and play behaviors. According to these theories, all individuals inherit the behaviors which allow them to participate in these tasks. Therefore, they show how to observe the behavior of one individual and compare it to the actions of other species members.

These theories contain words which direct attention toward external behavior as it is related to the species' tasks. Mating in humans would be an example of the focus demonstrated by ethological theories. Advocates of this type of theory are also interested in how individuals grow into demonstration of the types of behaviors related to the species' tasks.

Theories and Your Understanding of Child Development

Each of the four theories described above enables us to refine our abilities to understand children. You may prefer one more than the others. But, it is important to remember that each has its value by focusing our attention on different aspects of child development and by giving us different ways to think about children. We are probably better informed if we are familiar with all four theories than if we know only one.

As you study these theories, notice they will help you decide what you think. These theories can, in fact, help you develop your own theory about children and how they develop. You might never become a researcher or a scientist in a formal sense. But, you might become a parent or a teacher. Do you think it is important to have a theory about children and how they develop? What if your theory is too limited and you have some notions which are not true? What will the consequences be for the children? What if you have a variety of ways to think about children? Will you likely do a better job of understanding and predicting what children will do?

The answers to these questions are pretty obvious, aren't they? This implies, however, that as you acquire knowledge about these theories and about children that you should examine your assumptions and decide what parts of human behavior you want to consider. Are you more interested in observable external behavior than you are in mental development? Or are you equally concerned about thoughts, emotions, and acts?

The theories provide a way to understand children and also provide specific knowledge about them. You can use them to formulate your own theory and improve your ability to promote healthy human development. ❀

Innate Needs

The root that nourishes all human relationships is the principle of stewardship. Stewardship is a charge to care for and nurture others. Stewardship implies an accounting to someone. Sometimes we are accountable to entities in this life. Parents often have to account for their stewardship to schools, welfare agencies, churches, and the law. For instance, if parents are not good stewards and neglect children, the state may take the children out of the home and place them in foster care. It always comes as a shock to people to find out that their children do not legally belong to them. They belong to the state in which they live. You could test this notion out. Abuse a child and see what happens. If the state knows about it, the child will be taken away from you while people try to train you to be more nurturing. If you can't or won't change your behavior, then your child might be permanently taken from you. So, legally, children don't belong to parents. This means parents can't do whatever they want with their children.

To be a good steward over children, a person has to accept the notion that each child is unique. It is unfair for parents to think all their children are the same and try to fit all of them into the same mold.

The uniqueness of children comes from several sources. First, children are unique because of their genetic inheritances. Everyone is genetically different unless he or she is an identical twin. Science is just beginning to discover some of the subtle personality traits that heredity influences. For instance, whether a person is impulsive or reflective seems to be largely determined by genes.

The second source of uniqueness comes from the environment. The environment includes everything that happens to a person from the moment he or she is conceived. Everyone has had a unique environment. It is impossible to create the same environment for two people. Sometimes parents of twins try to make their children's lives identical, but it is impossible. They can dress them alike, give them names that sound alike, and even put them side by side in a double-seated stroller so that they go through life seeing new things at the same time, but their environment is still not the same.

Most children do the same things over a long period of time. All children get angry with their parents. They all have temper tantrums and display negative behavior. Children do the same things, but not at the same time.

Child A has a talent for throwing a temper tantrum just as the family comes home from church when everyone is feeling pretty mellow. The mother says to herself, "I can understand this behavior, he's just growing up. Bless his little heart. He's in a stage. He'll grow out of it." The behavior of Child A is seen through rose-colored glasses by the mother.

But another child, Child B, does the same thing five minutes before her mother has an appointment. Her temper tantrum makes the mother late. The mother interprets the behavior, which is the same as Child A's, through different-colored glasses and reacts to her differently. Then an interesting thing happens. The mother starts to see Child B as a bad child and tunes into bad behaviors more often, interpreting more and more of that child's behavior as bad. She may label the child as bad and then look for confirmation in her "bad" behavior. And she can find it. She will ignore the good things that the child does. Some of you know what I am talking about because you were assigned such a label in your family. The opposite happens with Child A.

Once a parent gives a child a label, the other brothers and sisters catch on and use the label. Check this out. Next time your family gathers together, have everyone write down three adjectives that describe each person. You might be surprised at how much agreement there is between your brothers and sisters. Usually, everyone in a family knows the roles that everyone else is supposed to play. This happens with both good and bad traits.

It has also been observed by many psychologists that children are born with similar needs and internal forces that push them to seek similar goals. These have been called innate needs. Innate needs have been found to be the same in all children in every culture. They are independent of the culture in which a child is raised. Children do not acquire these needs; they are born with them. But they do not come from the child's genes. These needs cannot be accounted for by environmental or genetic factors. So where do they come from? Psychologists have yet to determine the answer to this question.

The list of innate needs is not lengthy. Yet each of these innate needs is like an empty bucket that needs to be filled. When the bucket, or need, is full, a person is happy. Unfortunately, every bucket has a hole in the bottom. No matter how often a child's bucket is filled, if a parent relaxes and thinks, "Well, that is taken care of," and stops filling the bucket, then the bucket will eventually drain dry, and the child will again seek to satisfy the unmet need.

Suppose that someone takes you to the local Taco Bell for lunch. You eat four burritos, which should fill up anybody. Then this person orders four more for you to eat. You eat one more but can't eat the rest, and so this person forces you to eat the other three burritos. At this point you say, "One more bite and I will throw up!" This person asks, "Are you full?" and you say, "YES!" Then the person says, "Good, no more food for a month." You know that won't work. Your bucket for physical food is overflowing, but in three hours, you will probably be hungry again. The same analogy holds for each of the needs we are going to discuss. They need constant replenishment.

When a need is not filled, some interesting things happen. First, a subconscious level tries to give the child a message to do something. It tries to bring about change. Sometimes a child does this through attention-getting behavior. Some believe that most of the hyperactivity in elementary school children is caused by one or more of their innate needs not being met. When children act out, they are sending a message to teachers and parents that they need help. If the undirected attention-getting behavior does not work, then a second event usually happens. The child gives up and a depression sets in.

Many adults have grown up with some of their needs only partially filled and, as a result, are not totally healthy in some area of their development such as intellectual, moral, or social development. Adults can fill their own buckets; they can heal themselves. If a person feels intellectually stunted, he or she can take a class and learn something new. If a person is physically out of shape, she or he can take up jogging or aerobics and get fit. Adults can fill their own needs. Only in the most severe cases of neglect might a person need help from someone else such as a physician, counselor, teacher, or minister. You cannot fill another person's bucket if your own is dry. Parents should make sure they are healthy before they start to work with their children. If they are not healthy, they may not even be able to see the needs that their children have. In childhood, some buckets have such big holes that the buckets have to be filled up every day.

Let's discuss some of the important innate needs. This list is not exhaustive but includes most of the currently recognized innate needs. The first need is the need to stay alive. This is perhaps the most powerful need that we have because when this need is not met, a person physically dies and doesn't have to worry about the other needs. A medical friend of mine has suggested that you only need six things to survive: food, air, water, sleep, removal of waste products from your body, and maintenance of your body temperature. It is interesting that newborn babies can only do three of these things for themselves. They need to have a caretaker provide their food and water and help maintain their body temperature.

There seems to be a time in the course of many people's lives when they realize they have accomplished all they can and no longer struggle to maintain life. It often happens when people are old and have lived a good life. Younger people cannot understand it.

Dylan Thomas is a good example. His father was dying and apparently in the condition I have just described, willing to die. His father's attitude was disturbing to Dylan, and so he lamented:

> *Do not go gentle into that good night,*
> *Old age should burn and rave at close of day;*
> *Rage, rage against the dying of the light.*
>
> *Though wise men at their end know dark is right,*
> *Because their words had forked no lightning they*
> *Do not go gentle into that good night...*
>
> *And you, my father, there on the sad height,*
> *Curse, bless me now with your fierce tears, I pray.*
> *Do not go gentle into that good night.*
> *Rage, rage against the dying of the light.*

Dylan thought his father should struggle to stay alive. From Dylan's perspective, he should be struggling to maintain life.

Man does not live by bread alone, however. We have several other needs to care for. The following needs are just as powerful as the need to stay alive. When they are not met, the physical body does not die, but a person "dies" intellectually, spiritually, morally, or socially.

Children Have a Need To Gain Knowledge

The nine months a fetus is in the womb is the dullest part of one's whole existence. After nine months of this environment, the baby is willing and anxious to be born. Doctors do not have to coax babies out of the womb. Children want to learn.

Unfortunately, a lot of parents unwittingly deprive their children of stimulation and the chance to fill this need after they are born. They put their children in cribs or infant seats for the bulk of the day. An infant seat is a marvelous thing, but it pins the children's arms down to their sides so they can't move. It also has a plastic protector that wraps around the sides of the child's head. It is like blinders on a horse. It limits what children can see. All they can do is look straight ahead. Children in an infant seat may sit for hours on the kitchen counter beside their mother as she does her chores for the day, and all they can do is look straight ahead at the side of a lime-green refrigerator. There is not a lot of stimulation in that. What happens to a child who is stimuli deprived? The child gets restless.

When children learn to crawl at six or seven months of age, nature says, "Go." And children start to explore. They get into the pots and pans cupboard. They get into their mother's purse. They get into everything. These are not bad children. They are children with healthy spirits. They are children who want to learn and make up for lost time. These small children are kind of like the wolf in *Little Red Riding Hood*. When they find a new object, they fondle it with their hands ("The better to feel you with"), they may put it in their ears ("The better to hear you with"), or their mouth ("The better to taste you with"), or their nose ("The better to smell you with"), and so on. One of my daughters was thirteen months old at Thanksgiving one year. She was sitting in her high chair. On the table in front of her, within her reach, was a bowl of peas. She had never eaten real peas before. She got her hands on some peas and found she could roll them around on her high chair tray. Then she found that they fit up her nose. She started pushing peas up one of her nostrils as fast as she could go. Why do children do things like that? Why do they put things in their ears and nose, and bad tasting stuff in their mouths? These are ways to learn about the new object. Children use all five of their senses to learn about the world.

If children are not having this need met, they will try to get someone's attention who can intervene on their behalf and fulfill this need. Many of you will have children who will struggle to fill this need. This struggle often happens in the midst of plenty at school. In America, we believe in educating everyone. That is the democratic way. Many other countries do not educate everyone, but we try to. When you educate every child, you have to use a curriculum that is at the level of the average child.

A public school curriculum is geared to the pace of three-time learners. But, in classrooms there are one-time learners and five-time learners, and their needs will not be met with that curriculum. They are bored or lost, and they often resort to attention-seeking behaviors to see if someone will give them a curriculum that will meet their needs. Teachers don't have time to reach the few very slow or very fast, and so parents have to pick up the slack and become active in educating their children.

Most fifth graders have spelling every day. They get a list of twenty-five new spelling words and practice these words at their desks on Monday and Tuesday. Then on Wednesday, they might have a pretest to see how well they are doing. On Thursday they might practice the words they missed on Wednesday. On Friday they would have the real test. In this arrangement, they practiced the words three times, on Monday, Tuesday, and Thursday. What if the teacher told them that if the whole class scored one hundred percent on the spelling test, they could have a party? Most classes would never have a party because there will be at least two students who are five-time learners. They will never get it. They will just about get the words, but then it would be Monday of a new week, and they would get the new list of words to learn.

There will also be one or two one-time learners in this class. They will be so smart that they can read through the list of words on Monday and have them learned. They will want to do other things during spelling time the rest of the week but the teacher will say, "No." Discipline problems in this class will include the one-time learners and the five-time learners. One group is bored and the other is lost, but the problem is the same, even though it doesn't seem that way on the surface. The need to learn is not being met.

Children Have a Need To Make Order and Sense out of Their Experiences

This need is expressed in many ways. It is one thing for a person to have a rich learning environment and learn new things, but it is quite another to make sense out of these experiences. But something inside propels people to try to do it. This need can be seen in very young children. When children are taken to adult activities they do not understand what is going on. Their world becomes a world of nonsense.

Small children struggle to make some sense out of what they experience. Children twist things around until they make a little sense. You have all seen examples of this. It shows up in the funny little things that children say. For instance, "I pledge allegiance to the flag of the United States of America,...one naked individual...with liver and tea for all." The words "nation indivisible" and "liberty" don't mean anything to children, and so their minds twist them around into something that sounds familiar.

The lessons children learn as they are growing are not presented to them in an orderly fashion. Take, for instance, the television program *Sesame Street*. In an average episode, there may be as many as thirty different, short learning episodes. And few, if any of them, will be related. There may be a small section in which they will learn a number. A voice in the TV says aloud, "One, two, three, four, five, five, five, FIVE." This is accompanied by a picture of five Indians, five bicycles, and five ice cream cones on the screen. Then that episode is over and four pictures will appear on the screen. Three are alike and one is different and the child is asked to identify the different one. And then there may be a discussion of "near" and "far." None of the episodes are related. At the end of *Sesame Street*, the producers will try and make it look like there was something cohesive about the program by saying something like, "The program was brought to you today by the letters, B, Y, U, and the number 5."

Children have many small, unrelated learning bursts, and they don't know how to organize and make sense out of these experiences. It is a little bit like asking a person to put together a giant jigsaw puzzle without showing the picture. It would be very difficult because, while they have all the pieces, they don't know what to do with them. They don't know if they are putting together a flower garden or a horse race because each piece is so small that it doesn't make sense. It is the same way in life. Someone has to help children see the big picture and help them fit each new experience into the total picture. Parents are that someone.

Children Have a Need To Be in Control of Their Lives

Everyone wants to make decisions and be in control. You can see this in very young children. If they don't get to make decisions, this bucket goes dry and they may resort to undesirable behavior. When parents with young children insist on making every decision for them such as what clothes they can wear, when they go to bed, and what they can eat, they are going to see some very negative behavior in their children. Their children may get very stubborn and resist control. They may fight back and rebel against their parents. Something inside of children makes them want to be in control of their lives by making choices. You can fill this bucket in little children by letting them make choices as simple as dressing themselves and feeding themselves. You cannot let children make all their decisions, however, because they are not wise enough.

The other side of this need is that when people get to make choices, they have to be responsible for those choices. It is common to give children choices and then let them off the hook when they make a mistake. This is not a good idea. It teaches irresponsibility. It also demeans children. Children almost always interpret such acts of mercy as a lack of confidence by the parent. Therapists and counselors tell us that when parents finally say to a child who has never had to be responsible, "We are going to make you be responsible for this act," it becomes the turning point in that child's life to getting back to "normal." This is sometimes called "tough love."

The guiding principle for parents who are trying to fill this need in their children is to ask themselves this question: "If I give my children a choice and they make the wrong choice, am I willing to make them be responsible?" If parents honestly don't think they can do that, they shouldn't give children the choice in the first place. You do more damage letting children make a choice and then not making them be responsible for the choice than you do by being dictatorial and not letting children make a choice.

Children Have a Need To Be Close to Others

Closeness can be filled in several settings including the closeness inside families and the closeness with friends. Families are the first social institutions that children come in contact with. If a family is nurturing and takes care of an infant, children will feel like they belong and will bond to the family. The earliest bonding experience is close physical contact with caretakers. It is appropriate and desirable for a young child to be handled, cuddled, caressed, tickled, hugged, and snuggled. Such physical contact bonds children to their caretakers. Humans never outgrow this need for close physical contact.

Close physical contact is not sexual in nature. People who try to fill the empty bucket for closeness through sexual contact never fill the bucket. No matter how sexually active they are, their spirits never get happy. That is why people who are sexually promiscuous are never satisfied but are always searching for another conquest. Non-sexual physical closeness is more satisfying.

As children get older, there are other things parents can do to help them bond to the family. These activities involve sharing with a child. Sharing experiences with a child is good, but the greatest glue for bonding children to families is to share feelings with them. In today's hectic world this is hard to do because parents don't spend a lot of time with children, and so they have very few opportunities to share feelings.

The emotions family members share don't always have to be positive. In our society of mobile, nuclear families, the main shared emotional experience is usually grief at the death of a relative. When a death is unexpected or violent, the grief becomes more intense and its bonding potential increases. But, any strong emotion can bond people together.

Emotions don't have to be experienced together by parent and child. A parent can share an emotion vicariously with the child. It is a good practice for parents to share with their children emotional events from their own pasts.

Bonding cannot occur without spending time with the child. We often hear the term, "quality time." Some people use this as an excuse for not spending more time with their children. They say, in essence, "I'm not home much, but when I am, I'm really great." You cannot reduce the amount of time you spend with your child down to five minutes of red hot quality time. Not only do you have to have quality time, but you also need to spend a lot of time with each child. A good guideline of how much time is at least fifteen minutes a day for each child, one-on-one.

Children realize that it is an act of love when parents share their resources with them. The more scarce the resources that are shared, the more children perceive the sharing as being an act of love. They feel valued in their parents' eyes. In some families, the scarcest resource will be money. If a poor family gave a child its last dollar, that would be seen as an act of love. In middle-class families, the giving of money is not usually seen as the same thing. Giving money may take away some guilt from a parent, but it is not an act of love. The scarcest commodity in middle-class families is time. Spending time with a parent is more precious than gold to a child. You have to give children enough of your time so they recognize that you have shared with them. If children do not feel a closeness to their family, they will seek for bonding in other places. The group they decide to bond with may not be a group you like. You will want to spend a lot of time bonding with your children.

Children Have a Need To Achieve

Achievement means that a child wants to be special and outstanding in some way. A child can feel this by something as simple as having the best bug collection or being the best reader in a class. Middle-class parents are pretty good at praising and encouraging their children, but the praise usually comes in only three areas of activity: academic activities (How well are children doing in school?), athletic activities (Are they on an athletic team?), and cultural activities (Can they tap dance and play the flute?). If children take lessons in these areas, they will get better. Parents send their children to summer camps and give them lessons so that they will be good at something. Excellence in any of those areas will certainly fill this need. A child that is a great student knows that she is a great student and gets a lot of satisfaction from that knowledge. If a child is a good athlete, people will let him know it.

Unfortunately, many children cannot excel in any of these areas. They have talents in other areas. Such children are usually ignored by their parents and not given the opportunity to excel because their parents aren't aware of what to look for in them. Some talents parents might look for are interpersonal in nature such as leadership, compassion, love, listening, and empathy.

It would be amazing if some night at the dinner table a parent turned to a child and said, "You are the most loving child in our family and I just want you to know that we appreciate it." The very idea sounds odd when you see it in print, but it is no more odd than when a parent talks about the grades or athletic accomplishments of children who are gifted in those areas. Parents should identify some areas in which their children can achieve and then give them practice opportunities and praise so they can improve. It is important to let older children in a family know of the talents of the younger children. It gives the younger children status with their siblings.

Children have a need to share with others and to serve others. It is one thing to have a lot of talents, but it is another to move outside ourselves and share them. When people become totally egocentric and hoard their talents for use by themselves or a small group of friends, they wither away psychologically. Their buckets go dry and they are not happy. Humans need to serve and share with people. The sharing that works best is when other people do not know about it. It is not like when a group of friends divide up and pick secret friends for whom they do nice things and at the end of the month reveal everyone's secret friend. In such situations, children are more concerned about getting recognition for being the giver than about the act of sharing. It is more like the Sub-for-Santa model in which volunteers do things anonymously. No Sub-for-Santa person would think about going back to a family in July and asking, "Did you like what you got for Christmas last year? We are the ones that gave it to you." Parents need to find opportunities for their children to do good things.

Children Have a Need To Learn How To Receive Things

Isn't this interesting? We teach our children that they should be independent, stand on their own, and not depend on anyone. We teach them that they are the masters of their own fates. But inside, the child knows that people have to live cooperatively and that involves giving and taking. Most people don't know how to receive and they feel uncomfortable doing it. There is nothing more boorish than a person who cannot receive a gift graciously.

A parent has to set the example of interdependence. We have heard angry parents say to their children, "I don't need you! You need me and don't you forget it." In a healthy family, this would never happen. A parent should say, "I need you, I need this kind of thing from you, and I recognize that you need some things from me."

We need each other. We need to foster mutually dependent relationships. "No man is an island," as John Donne wrote.

Children Need Solitude

Solitude means time to be alone. Healthy people need about thirty minutes each day to be psychologically and physically alone. During this time, they can make plans, review the day, commune with nature, pray, or write in a journal. When people get so busy that they don't have that time, they will be neither healthy nor happy. Sometimes, students get themselves into such a fix. They take too many classes. Successful business people who are workaholics are not happy. They never have time to relax and think. The need for solitude is not filled. So they work even harder to accomplish more and feel satisfied.

What they really need is to be less driven and more relaxed. Being over-programmed goes against the grain of human nature.

Children Have a Need for Beauty and To Be Surrounded by Beautiful Things

Beauty is not always in the eye of the beholder. The same things appear beautiful to many people. Many agree that certain paintings are beautiful, for instance. A healthy soul likes to be around beautiful things in music, art, and nature. A family should gather beautiful things and memories around them. There is something worthwhile about putting money, time, and energy into making the surroundings that your children are growing up in attractive and beautiful. You do not have to be rich to have beautiful things. Being expensive and ornate does not necessarily make something beautiful.

That is the basic list of innate needs. It is not the exhaustive list. There are probably a few innate needs that we have not listed, but at the beginning we gave you the generic description so you could recognize any innate need. When you see the same need in every child, in every culture, and the need remains throughout a person's lifespan, you are probably looking at an innate human need.   ❀

Principles of Development

There are several general principles of development that can help a person understand how children grow and how all systems work together. When we understand that the same basic principles are influencing several areas of development, it appears children grow according to some overall design.

Principle One: *In those areas of development influenced by heredity, heredity sets the upper limits on what can be achieved.* Once our genetic potential is set at the moment of conception, there is nothing we can do to raise that potential. For instance, we all have a genetic potential for intelligence, and neither special instruction, nor diets, nor exercise can help a person achieve beyond that potential.

Principle Two: *Learning waits for maturation.* This means that when you have a child practice to develop a skill, all the practice is wasted until the child is mature enough to benefit from the training. Research has shown that if you take identical twins who have the same genetic potential and give one of them practice in crawling up stairs from the time he is very young, and the other twin is given no practice, the second twin will crawl up stairs within a couple of days after the first one has learned how.

The reason for this is that all the practice with the first twin was useless until the brain and muscle system were mature enough to make use of it. Once the twin was mature enough, then the practice really paid off. When mature, the child learned very rapidly, and since the twin matured at the same time, when placed on the stairs the second child learned with just a few trials. Parents need to get a sense of their children's periods of maturation to help them be realistic about what their children can accomplish. If a child isn't mature enough, then parents should relax and not push lessons on a child.

Principle Three: *The environment acts as a drag upon potential.* While it is impossible to raise somebody's genetic potential, there are many things that can lower that potential. In the case of intelligence, a high fever, some diseases, and head injuries can all lower the potential. Once the potential has been lowered by environmental factors, it is difficult or impossible to restore it.

Principle Four: *Development is orderly.* While it may not seem so to a casual observer, there is a design to how children grow into adults. One of the orderly processes is called the cephalo-caudal principle. It states that a child grows from the head toward the foot. Another closely related principle is called the principle of proximo-distal development. This states that a child matures from the central part of the body (the spinal column) out toward the periphery (toes and fingers).

In the chart on the following page, the horizontal axis represents an increase in age from birth to maturity and the vertical axis represents how mature somebody is (immature at birth until fully mature as an adult). The straight line shown in the graph is a phenomenon that never happens. If it were a true phenomenon, it would mean that for every week, month, or year that a child lives, he or she increases the same amount in whatever area he or she is developing (e.g., two inches every year, five pounds every year, six IQ points every year, etc.). There is nothing that operates this way.

Principle Five: *While development is orderly in each system, there are periods of rapid and slower development.* The other curves in the graph show some of the typical ways that children grow. Notice that in Curve A the child is mostly mature by the time he or she is four and very little development takes place after that.

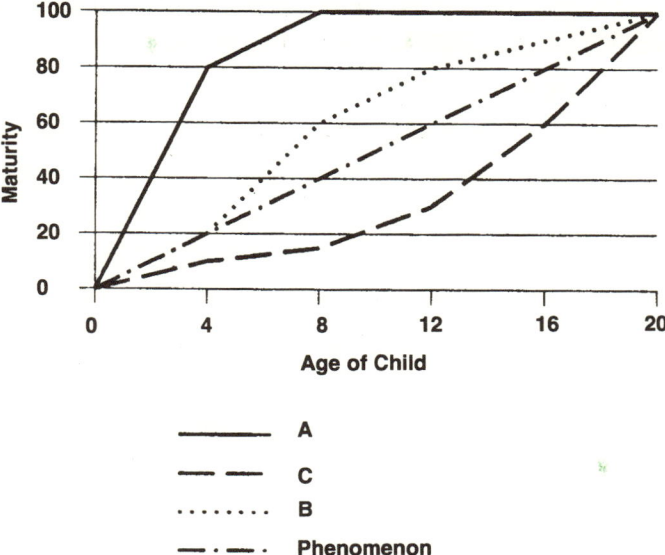

In Curve C, very little development occurs for the first twelve or so years of life. Then there is some rapid development, and within a period of two or three years, the person is mature.

Principle Six: *Different systems in a child follow different growth curves.* Not all systems experience periods of rapid growth at the same time.

Principle Seven: *In normal, healthy children the sequence of development is always the same.* The timing of development can vary widely, but the sequence is the same. Hence, all children learn to sit up before they learn to crawl, they learn to crawl before they learn to walk, and they learn to walk before they learn to run and skip. But different children learn to walk at different ages and they spend different amounts of time in each stage.

Principle Eight: *In each of the systems which develop in a child, there are critical periods.* A critical period is usually a time of rapid change, when the curve is the steepest in the chart. During critical periods a child is particularly susceptible to environmental influences for both good and bad, so parents should be vigilant during those critical periods in order to give children the proper guidance, to help them develop correctly, and to protect them, especially from harmful events that could throw them off track.

Principle Nine: *Children have a built-in catch-up system.* If a child is not developing properly due to environmental factors such as illness or stress, and the problem is eliminated, the child will develop faster than normal for a period until he or she makes up the developmental ground lost. In other words, children catch up to where they were supposed to have been (remember that they cannot exceed their genetic potential—Principle One).

In the diagram on page 45, the solid line represents genetic potential. The dotted line represents how they are actually developing. Notice that around Point A something in the environment causes them to develop below their potential. If someone intervenes in the environment between Point A and Point B and corrects the event that pulled the child off the developmental curve, the child will grow faster than expected and get right back up to his or her potential.

Such a time period exists in just about all phases of development. The length of time between Point

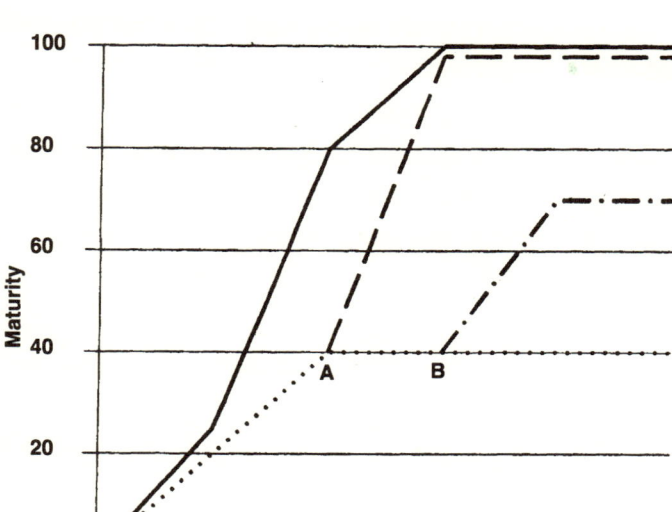

A and Point B varies with each system and between people. If a person waits past Point B to intervene and intervenes between Points B and C, there will be a partial catching up. The closer the intervention takes place to Point B, the more a child will catch up; the closer to Point C, the less. For some systems, there is a point of no return. If you wait past Point C to intervene in a child's environment, catching up will not take place at all. For some systems in human development, there is no Point C. It should be a source of comfort to prospective parents to know that when something interferes in a child's development and alert parents become aware of it, they can do something that will help their child reach his or her full potential.

Principle Ten: *All systems are coordinated in their development.* In the earlier graph, notice that while some systems were growing fast, others were more or less dormant. Then, those roles were reversed. Apparently, humans do not have enough energy to grow rapidly on all systems at the same time.

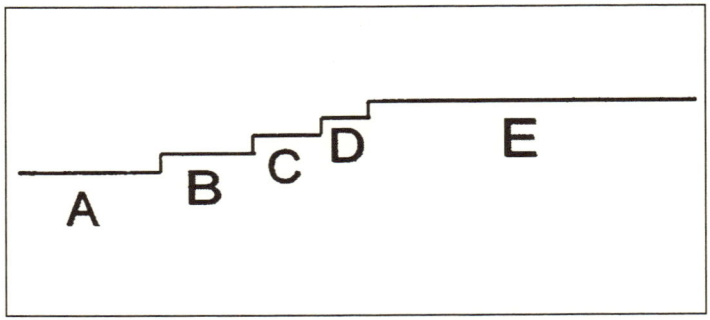

Principle Eleven: *As children mature, they go through certain stages when little progress is made.* There will be periods of rapid change mingled with more stable states. Sometimes the change is very dramatic and sometimes it is not. Sometimes a stage lasts for a long time and sometimes for a short time. The diagram above depicts what this looks like. Plateau A is of average length, Plateau B is below average, Plateau C is much below average, Plateau D is even shorter, and then Plateau E is very long. The concept of stages is very useful and there are two insights that are associated with it.

The first insight is that children always want to be a stage or two ahead of where they are. When children are preschoolers they want to go to school and when children are school age they want to do the things adolescents do. Parents who don't know any better let their children get away with this, but a good parent will make children stay in each stage until they have matured and accomplished what they need to do in each of those stages. This means that if a family has several children with a wide age range, the parents will be very busy organizing experiences that are appropriate to each child's age. It is very difficult to have a meaningful family night with children that are both very young and very old because children of different stages have different kinds of needs and experiences.

One way to visualize children's stages is to picture that a child at each stage is like a different animal on a farm. Instead of the letters A, B, C, D, and E on the diagram, you could write "cow," "pig," "horse," "chicken," and "goat." A farmer cannot go to the feed store and say, "I want a ton of chicken feed" and expect all of the animals to like it. All animals have different diets, different kinds of exercise, and different things they need to do. That's what children are like.

The second insight is that parents have favorite children, just like farmers always have favorite animals. They may love all the animals equally, take care of all of them, and appreciate their value to the farm, but they have favorites and so do parents. It is just about impossible for a parent to be psychologically in tune with each different stage of childhood. Some parents relate well to infants. Others are soulmates with school-age children, and others get along excellently with adolescents. Often a child who is in a stage that a parent understands well becomes the parent's favorite. Parents do not need to apologize for this. What they need to do is recognize it, and then avoid acting as if they have favorites. To have a favorite does not mean that you do not love, care for, and appreciate your other children.

Principle Twelve: *Children's minds always race ahead of their bodies.* Children can picture doing things that they are not physically capable of doing (e.g., a two year old wanting to ride a bike). Since this is a principle with adults as well, we can see it in our own lives. All of us can picture ourselves doing things such as being great athletes, but our bodies won't respond. For a healthy adult, a failure like this is not devastating because we realize we have other strengths.

When a child doesn't feel competent and has low self-esteem, failure becomes very frustrating. A typical example would be children who want to draw a picture for their mother. They laboriously draw the picture and after spending many minutes on it, suddenly rip it up and throw it away. The reason they do this is because their minds can see what they want to draw but their bodies won't do it. If their parents are supportive of the artistic efforts and reward the process of drawing instead of the product, frustration will be less.

Principle Thirteen: *The process of development is more important than the product of development.* In school, a teacher might give the class an assignment to learn about the state they live in. The teacher grades final papers on how much information they contain, how neat they are, and so on. This is a product-oriented teacher. Alternatively, a teacher could realize that the most important thing is to teach a process of how to find information, synthesize it, organize it, and present it. Such a teacher does not care much about the end result, but judges pupils on the kind of progress they are making. When parents have this attitude, they will never compare one child to another. As long as a child is on the right developmental path and headed in the correct direction, they know that the child will eventually reach the goal. They know that some children will go faster than others, so it does not become a concern. They don't compare the child to other children.

Principle Fourteen: *The principle of correlations, or, as someone once put it, "Them that has, gets!"* This is the opposite of the principle of compensation, which most people seem to believe. The law of compensation says that if children are gifted in some area such as intelligence, then they will be deficient in another area. You have heard statements like, "Beautiful, but dumb," or "Smart, but awkward." Compensation is not the true principle. The true principle is that those people who have received great genetic potential in one area seem to be above average in nearly every other area. The bad side of the coin is that the opposite is also true. When children are handicapped in some area, they are usually multiply handicapped. We speak of syndromes, whole clusters of things that go together. Good things go with good things; bad things go with bad things. However, no matter how handicapped children are, each has some area in which to excel. This is very hard for most psychologists to explain. The main character in the movie *Rainman* is an example of this.

Principle Fifteen: *Children grow best in the shade.* This is just a cute way of saying that children develop and flourish when they are in the protective shadow, or shade, of a parent or caretaker who loves and watches them and is close enough to be aware of what is going on in their lives.

Principle Sixteen: *Children seek for fulfillment.*

Principle Seventeen: *Children can learn to cope with nearly any environment that is consistent.* ❀

Developmental Tasks

Most of us love our children and find them fascinating. Sometimes we look at them and feel we cannot get enough to fill our eyes or our hearts. There seems to be no end to the remarkable things children say and do. For those who have more than one child, they discover that the first has taught them to be more observant of the second. I recall a friend telling me that he and his wife decided to place their new baby's crib at the foot of their bed so they could notice everything about him. "We learned," he said, "that we missed a lot of things with the other kids." He and his wife had eight children.

We must do more than watch them or pay attention just to see the new and enjoyable things they do. We must watch them to understand their maturation. Watching children to see their growth and progress is called a "developmental perspective." We can enjoy them all we can, but in addition, the developmental perspective means to have a view of childhood that stretches from before birth to adulthood. It means that we try to understand where our children have come from, what they are doing now, and how they will develop later.

Imagine that you can see in one moment someone's past, present, and future. At any moment you could understand what a child has been like, what the child is now doing, and what would happen later. That knowledge and perspective would guide your thoughts and actions to help your children in a way your limited vision of the present and past cannot.

I remember watching one of my sons play basketball. As a former player, I watched him miss opportunities because he had not learned to play with his left hand. Later, when we played together, I defended his right hand so he had to use his left. At first he was awkward but gradually became better. Later, at one of his games, I watched as he turned to survey his options, hesitated just for a moment, and then used his left hand to score a basket. I felt a thrill of fulfillment although I never told him what I had been doing. I just saw how he needed to develop and helped him do it. I was older and understood what he would need. That experience was far more rewarding than his basketball successes.

Of course, we are not omniscient and cannot see all that will happen. As a result, our understanding is less than complete. Yet we can see much about a child's future if we are willing to pay attention. After all, we were once children and we have developed and grown. Besides, watching one child go through several stages improves our abilities with those that come later. The point is, that focusing on the development of our children is simply the best perspective to help us formulate an effective child care and management plan. It is the best perspective because it is realistic. It is what really happens, whether we care to notice or not. By noticing, we can use our knowledge to make ourselves into the kind of parents we would like to be and find many rewards in the bargain.

Understanding some things about the way children develop lets us apply the primary parenting principle. We can monitor their development and help them or get out of the way. In my experience this is the least used but most valuable information available to parents. Yet, many of us do not understand this principle clearly until our children are grown. Then we recognize what we wish we had known and done while they were young. This happens at the moment we think, "I wish I could start again," or "I wish I had known this earlier."

The Benefits of a Developmental Perspective

A developmental perspective is important for many reasons. First, it improves our abilities to understand our children. At any moment in time we can see what our children actually do and then link it to something we know is in their future. Some parents, for example, give gifts to their children that will please them now and will be even more interesting to them in the next year.

Second, it gives us more ideas about how to respond to our children. If we understand about child development, we will have a wider ranger of options in responding to what they do. A developmental perspective also provides more ideas about how to respond. In any situation with a child, we observe and then respond. Our choices of action will depend on our perspective. Suppose we have a rule-oriented perspective and think our primary task is to make and enforce rules. Our perspective will focus our attention on obedience and disobedience. If we think a child is breaking a rule, for instance, our obedience/disobedience orientation will present us with the decision to punish or not, and, if we punish, how to do it. This appears so logical that we think of little else. It might not occur to us that misbehavior is a sign that the child is ignorant of something. Here, misbehavior can be an opportunity to teach an important lesson. However, instead of using the opportunity to teach, we spend our energy punishing the child. We will have failed to use a more positive, effective approach.

Third, a developmental perspective helps parents be more positive, effective, and constructive. Working toward some positive future leads to hope, encouragement, and satisfaction. It is like the parents who discovered one day they could talk their children out of discouragement by getting them to pay attention to some positive future possibility. It not only helps the children, but gives hope to parents too.

A Developmental Perspective:
- **Improves your ability to understand**
- **Provides more ideas about how to respond**
- **Helps you be more positive and constructive**

Let us suppose you watched your child jump out of the bathtub and run around happily and excitedly without any clothes. Imagine that he or she likes doing this and does it as often as possible. What would you think? Is something wrong and should you do something to stop this behavior? Or, is this natural behavior for a two year old that can be safely ignored since he or she will grow into a sense of modesty? If you understood child development, you would be patient and amused because most children "run naked," but soon learn modesty as a natural part of childhood. In contrast, suppose at an older age this child hits, bites, and pinches until another child is hurt and cries. This is not a natural part of development and some action likely needs to be taken so the child learns an improved method of behaving.

Let us see the options a developmental perspective provides. In the face of aggression it is hoped you would not be indifferent and unresponsive, but what would you do? You understand that something is wrong, but why? Again, if you simply see this behavior as incorrect, which it is, you might devise a punishment designed to stop it. As some parents have, you might consider spanking or biting the child back if he or she bites you. That seems reasonable, doesn't it? It is not reasonable, and it is not effective since spanking and biting are acts of aggression. You will be rewarding the very actions you want to eliminate.

In contrast, if you have a developmental perspective, you will see beyond the misbehavior, recognize the signal that something is wrong, and correct it by promoting some growth or development. There are reasons for the behavior that must be found and resolved. Your solution could be to find the causes of the aggressive behavior. These might include experimentation, imitation, stress, or the lack of affection and warmth. Then you will need to teach a better form of behavior because, if uncorrected, your child will learn additional unhappy or unpleasant things. You might recognize any of the following:

1. The child might have been harshly treated by someone and may need more affection and warmth.

2. The child needs emotional comfort instead of harshness.

3. The child needs to learn more considerate ways of acting when unhappy (asking for comfort or being required to practice helping and kindness).

This example illustrates that a developmental perspective allows us to advance beyond mere punishment and to actually correct misbehavior. Misbehavior is a signal that something is wrong and needs to be solved. A lasting solution will be to teach the child a correct form of behavior.

In addition to this, a developmental perspective also helps us understand how children are maturing. It gives us goals that we can help our children achieve. Some parents mistakenly promote the growth in children that satisfies some narrow or selfish parental purpose. They may want their children to be helpless and dependent so they can feel powerful, or childish so they can retain the romantic notion of parenthood. If this growth were wholly good for the children little would be wrong with this idea. Frequently, however, such growth is not positive for the children because these parents think the children exist to love them or to live as their "toys." In these cases, a developmental perspective gives parents a reasonable view of child development that helps them balance their desires and what may be the best for the children.

Every Child Is Working On Developmental Tasks

Parents should be interested in promoting development for another reason. Continuing development is the central purpose of life for children. Nearly everything they do is related to some form of growth. Learning a developmental perspective simply allows parents to focus on children in the areas of their greatest interest. Someone once said, "Play is a child's work." I believe that play is as important as that statement suggests, but every child is engaged in a work more important than play. It is the achievement of some specific life lessons called "developmental tasks." These are the new abilities children are working toward—the improved, more mature characteristics we see emerge in them as they grow.

Imagine for a moment what this means. Children are around people who are more competent than they are, know more, can do more, and seem to function better in most ways. They understand that learning and developing is necessary. This "motivation" to grow is partly biological, too. Body and brain changes are a natural part of childhood. Change and development are central to every child's experience. Understanding developmental tasks is the most effective way to acquire a growth perspective. The idea about the existence of specific tasks has come from the research and countless hours of observations made by behavioral scientists. From this source, we learn that children are not passive individuals waiting for life to happen to them. They experiment, test, rehearse, and learn until they are successful. They adjust, adapt, repeat, and try again, and do so in at least five areas: mental, emotional, social, physical, and moral.

Our true responsibility as parents is to teach, motivate, regulate, and exemplify healthy and worthwhile behavior. This can only happen if parents focus on their children's learning and develop the parenting skills that will ensure it.

In the busy world we live in, many of us try to take short cuts in our parenting responsibilities. Because it is sometimes possible to conserve energy and effort, many try to rear children by relying on rules and by using some reward system. While both these methods are useful as disciplinary techniques, they are insufficient without the involvement parents give when they are committed to promote the development of their children.

One distinctive feature of high-quality parents is their skill in training and teaching correct or successful forms of behavior. We might hear one say, "My son has too little patience," or "He is an angry kid and we need to help him control that." They are focused on emotional, mental, social, moral, or physical behavior. They are committed to help their children learn and they organize and use their leadership to ensure this takes place.

Contrast this with parents who emphasize such goals as popularity, attractiveness, or high grades. All these have merit, but these goals can be focused on and even achieved with accompanying efforts on our part to help children achieve the behavior that produces them. It is all right to seek popularity, for example, if parents are willing to teach the positive social skills that might produce it. Attractiveness is also acceptable if some healthy and worthwhile behavior goes along with it. High grades will result if we concentrate our efforts on self discipline, persistence, and organization. Achieving these forms of development is the real goal of parenting.

Parents are "behavioral coaches" who have the most intimate contact with their children. Therefore, they have the most responsibility for teaching their children appropriate and useful behavior. No teacher, friend, sibling, or church leader shares in this expectation. When we focus on our responsibility and learn skills to achieve it, parenthood is the most fulfilling part of life. Some developmental tasks take many years to complete though we can see children begin them very early in life. Learning language is an example. Infants make vowel sounds when they coo and babble. They learn words, connect them to voice inflections, and use them in simple and then more complex sentences. Still, language development continues over many years and constantly improves if we continue to teach it.

Other tasks can be achieved in a shorter period and are specific to each stage of childhood. For example, infants are working to turn over, crawl, and walk. They do all these in a matter of months. Like language, however, achieving these and other similar skills is the work to which children give genuine effort and intent. In nearly every case, if you are interested enough and willing to learn, you can observe what your children are doing and help them be successful.

Completing Biological or Inherited Tasks

Some developmental tasks are inherited. Everyone, for example, continues to grow until he or she completes or achieves a mature height and body shape. Other less obvious tasks might include development of certain types of intelligence such as mathematics and logic, music, and art.

Many people fail to fully appreciate the power of inherited developmental tasks. In fact, even to this day some parents continue to think that everything about a child is learned from experience. An abundance of scientific evidence suggests that much of what happens to children is carried in the genes, as the following story illustrates.

A student was walking on the campus of a mid-western university. A girl approached him, smiled, called him an unfamiliar name and attempted to kiss him. He stopped and backed away. Surprised, he asked her what she was trying to do. She chided him for refusing her affection and told him he wasn't being funny. He protested again that he didn't know anyone by the name she had called him and said that she must be mistaken. Just as she was getting angry, a young man walked up to both of them who looked identical to the first young man. He called the girl by name, but could not stop staring at this "look-alike."

As the story unfolded, both men, who had been adopted, realized they were identical twins. Their story caught the attention of a newspaper reporter, and their picture was included as part of the story. Someone brought this article and picture to the attention of a third man living in a neighboring city. He was so similar to the other two in the picture that he called them. They all had the same haircut and shared many other interests. They were identical triplets, separated at birth, and placed in different adoptive homes.

This event sparked increased interest in the role our genetic background plays in our lives. Several attempts have been made to find others who share identical genetic backgrounds but did not share the same childhood environment. When they were located, the similarity between these individuals was startling. In one case, two brothers first learned of each other at age thirty-nine. They had a strong desire to meet. Their first meeting was astonishing. Both sported beards, wore similar clothes, weighed the same, had similar hobbies, worked in similar careers, married women with similar names, divorced, and remarried. They each had dogs with similar names.

Such accounts illustrate that a significant part of human development is determined genetically by our biological parents. The older children grow, the more influence their genetic code has in determining personality traits, career interests, talents, and many other abilities.

Further, inherited traits are a powerful force in shaping the course that development takes. Medical researchers, for example, have now demonstrated that humans inherit an internal clock that determines the rate and timing of physical growth. This means that some children grow rapidly while others do so gradually over a period. Some children have early growth spurts during puberty and others grow more slowly. We also inherit at least part of our emotional makeup because we know that at least five emotions are present at birth. Researchers have found surprise, disgust, anxiety, happiness/pleasure, and anger in every culture. This suggests that everyone inherits these emotions. We also inherit the ability to produce language sounds and interpret them into meaningful units. Brain researchers have found that we inherit our concepts of time, space, numbers, and the ability to classify or put ideas into categories. This shapes the way we think and learn and affects the emergence of our talents and abilities.

The fact that children have a "developmental code" built in when they are born—a genetic code that unfolds as they mature—should give parents considerable motivation to make sure that the code unfolds successfully and completely. The key word is "complete." We now better understand that if something is carried in the genetic makeup of a child, there is tremendous motivation to adjust, work, practice, and adapt until it is fully completed. This idea underlies the stories about very creative people who will work, sometimes under great opposition, to complete a project in order to satisfy the inner urge that motivates them. This same idea is the explanation for why bodies continue to grow and mature until that task is complete.

Let us examine several things that happen to children that are clearly the result of what they inherit. By examining these, you can see that our children come loaded with possibilities. For example, children do not need to formally practice walking. We have little to do with changes in hair color, the start of puberty, or the type of play children find interesting. Boys are more likely to enjoy rough and tumble play while girls prefer other forms of relational play. Significant aspects of children's mental abilities and emotional style unfold naturally, without much teaching or training from others. Parents play a vital role in whether children's biological tasks are completed.

In the last few years researchers have collected information that suggests the existence of more than one form of intelligence. Every individual may have some parts of all eight types but will obviously be more intelligent in some areas than in others. There is a strong biological factor that partly explains the origin and development of each person's intelligence. While reading about the types of intelligences described by Howard Gardner of Harvard University, think about yourself and your children. What forms of intelligence are prominent in each of you?

The Eight Intelligences

Musical/Rhythmic: The ability to understand combinations of blended sounds and to create or perform them. These sounds are used in composition, vocal, and instrumental performance.

Intrapersonal: Awareness of oneself including one's emotional life. This intelligence is usually demonstrated in helping professions and religious positions.

Social/Interpersonal: Understanding human relationships, social organizations, patterns of communication, and interaction. This intelligence may be observed in business, government, and other forms of social participation.

Logical/Mathematical: Understanding the rules of logic as applied to numbers and combinations of numbers. This intelligence is found in any task involving the manipulation of numbers and symbols.

Verbal/Linguistic: Understand words, what they mean, and how they are combined in order to communicate. This intelligence is applied in literature, poetry, and other forms of writing.

Visual/Spatial: Organizing objects in space. This intelligence is used in art and engineering.

Body/Kinesthetic: Ability in physical movement such as coordination and rhythm in dance or athletics.

Nature: Understand the environment, the outdoors, and living things.

Some of each intelligence can be observed in every child. There will be some motivation to develop all of them. However, when someone is especially endowed with one or more of these abilities there is tremendous motivation to completely fulfill them. It is as if great writers have books inside them waiting to be written so they can feel complete. Great dancers or athletes work to fully complete their abilities and are satisfied only when they sense or feel this completion. Individuals feel complete when they have fully and accurately described themselves and been understood or when they have made a satisfactory social contribution.

Intelligences and other inherited abilities are part of children's developmental tasks. Through them we see that all children have a similar goal, that is to fully and successfully complete what is within them. Their bodies and brains will not stop until they have finished their full biological measure. Think about how we can contribute to rather than become obstacles to our children. If we recognize our children's abilities, we can provide additional opportunities for them. We can stimulate, encourage, and motivate them to continue until their inherited abilities are complete. If we fail to recognize what our children bring with them we cannot help them as much. In addition, poor parenting means we offer little or nothing to help them in their efforts to complete their biological talents.

Achieving Competence

Children in the Fiji Islands have remarkable auditory memory. Scientists were puzzled at the children's astonishing abilities until the scientists learned that all traditions, rules, ceremonies, and family histories are passed orally by older people to their children. Thus, the Fiji children learned their histories, but also developed the sensory ability to be successful. This example, and many other situations like it, represents children's attempts to be competent in their own environment.

Polynesian navigators can observe natural signs and solve difficult and complex problems while navigating without instruments across thousands of miles of open ocean. Yet they perform poorly on written intelligence tests that have a Western cultural bias. Clearly this represents another example of people becoming competent in their environment.

Becoming competent in the outside world is the second kind of developmental task. Whereas inherited tasks are "built-in" and appear to have a motivation of their own to be completed, competence is achieved in the specific situations of childhood.

As with the motivation to complete inherited tasks, there is an intense motivation to gain competency. There are many recorded cases, for example, in which children learn criminal behavior, laziness, some forms of mental illness, and character problems because these behaviors were the ways to become "competent" in their environment.

On a more positive note, if they are required to become competent in a healthy, supportive environment, children will learn many helpful things. They improve on natural language abilities to communicate with others. They learn how to properly display inherited emotions to adapt and successfully "fit in" with other people and in certain situations. They search for the opportunity to express their talents. They practice to improve inherited physical skills, practice to become competent at music, and talk and visit with people until they have positive social relationships. They will work unsupervised if their project is interesting and will demonstrate their competence in whatever way possible.

Like completion, achieving competence is the basis of much childhood motivation. Those who help children become competent, therefore, will be highly valued and will have lifelong significance. This is why any involved parent, mentor, teacher, or friend has lasting influence. It is important for us as parents to distinguish between inherited abilities and the tasks at which children are learning to be competent. We might, for example, try to teach or require something children cannot do. We might fail to teach or provide expectations when we should. Further, unless we have a good understanding of the two types of tasks we might lend our confusion to our children.

For example, children are less likely to become competent if their environment requires them to do more than their inherited possibilities permit, or if inherited qualities are denied. In addition, it is possible that helplessness or incompetence might be fostered by a set of unpredictable or controlling conditions we supply in a child's environment. Children will, under the right conditions, learn these traits also.

When this happens, children do not fully complete their biological tasks or become competent individuals.

Yet, recognizing that children play a major role in their own development is important. They differ in their responses to the world. Some thrive when their families are a disaster of mistreatment, frustration, and discord. Others develop according to such dysfunctional conditions. In some families, children never match the expectations supplied by their family environment. They seem to lack the ability to do so. Others far exceed their conditions, defying the environment.

For us as parents, the best thing we can do is understand developmental tasks and know that we can positively influence how our children complete them. This idea is the essence of good parenting.

Helping Children Develop

An understanding of biological and environmental tasks helps us appreciate the real nature of childhood. Any observant parent can recognize and gain an appreciation for both. We admire and are sometimes in awe of the natural endowments our children bring with them. In other respects we are willing to work, teach, discipline, and train so that our children will become competent. In fact, we ourselves are still trying to complete inherited tasks and to gain competence in our world as we find it.

We must focus on our children in order to help them succeed. We must know and appreciate their inherited abilities and learn how to help them cultivate these abilities. Equally important, however, is that we create many of the early conditions children find in their environment. They will attempt to become competent in whatever environment we provide for them. This fact reaffirms our importance. Parents provide either a healthy family environment where children's development is encouraged or one where they find obstacles and difficulty.

Knowing about developmental tasks also enables us as parents to identify more specifically what we can and ought to do for our children. Instead of letting children grow by themselves like weeds in a vacant lot, we can influence and teach them. However, dominating them and occupying too great a place in their lives prevents them from becoming competent people. The best form of parenting is between these extremes.

As you begin to formulate a "parenting style" for yourself, consider what Lev Vygotsky, a Russian psychologist, thought. He acknowledged that children are born with their inherited abilities, which they seek to develop. He also recognized that parents offer the earliest and most instructive environment children ever know. He suggested that the two conditions create a "Zone of Proximal Development."

The range of development lies between what children bring with them and what conditions we supply. Consider the diagram on page 71. Think about this for a moment. Essentially, children will try to become competent at whatever conditions we create in our

---

Upper Level
Children's Environment
(What Parents Provide)

---

physical   emotional   mental

Zone of Proximal Development

language   social   moral

Lower Level
Biological Abilities
(What Children Inherit)

---

family environment. If we use high-quality language they will try to learn that type of language to communicate with us. If we use low-quality language, they will learn that. If we have excellent social skills, they will try to become competent in those areas, and so on.

Further, we have learned that if our family environment matches the children's inherited abilities they are likely to be more successful than if the environment is a serious mismatch. In many cases, whether children complete their tasks and become as competent as possible depends on whether they can find appropriate opportunities. That is, whether their experiences in learning match up with what they inherit. When this happy circumstance is realized, the results are usually remarkable.

Mozart's musical genius is legendary. His remarkable ability appeared early. At age four, he expressed irritation at and corrected other people's mistakes. These early abilities are evidence of inherited influences. Mozart's father and mother had strong music backgrounds and through their efforts created a fertile environment to match his inherited abilities. In him and others like him, we see the combination of inherited abilities matching up with opportunities to learn, producing extraordinary results. Even with different genetic possibilities, every child will benefit when natural abilities are matched with the right environment. Therefore, one skill we as parents will need is the ability to understand our children and organize a matching family environment.

Children do not work on all developmental tasks at the same time. They are trying to learn different qualities and abilities depending on their age. This means that part of your parenting style ought to include an understanding of children of different ages and stages so you can help them in each period of childhood. For example, children are born with the ability to look at, pay attention to, and respond to people. Language and emotional development give them improved social skills. Years later, going through puberty motivates them to become interested in heterosexual relationships. When it is time, they will leave to establish homes and families of their own. If they are successful, they will have completed their biological tasks and will have become competent during each of their life stages.

Also, understanding their tasks will help you identify their goals. Healthy parenting includes teaching, motivating, and preparing children for what is to come. This approach makes teaching and preparing much more important than trying to control. You will become your children's mentors—just what you ought to be. ❀

(This chapter is excerpted from *The Real Power of Parenthood: How to Find and Use It Successfully*, by A. Lynn Scoresby, Ph.D.)

Learning Disabilities

In this day and age, it is surprising that we are bare-ly discovering enough about learning disabilities to be of effective help. Even the people who are closest to the problem generally are still not informed about screening or identifying children with learning disabilities (LD). Therefore, many children are going through school feeling frustrated, being ridiculed, and becoming emotionally damaged because they think something is wrong with them. Something is wrong with children with learning disabilities, but it is not their fault. They are neither stupid nor deviant. They have learning disabilities which makes traditional learning experiences difficult and frustrating.

We used to think that learning disabilities were problems with the sensory system, so psychologists tested for visual, auditory, or motor deficits. Researchers finally demonstrated that learning disorders were cognitive, not sensory, and now our tests and procedures are designed to identify and help with cognitive problems. There are three types of learning disabilities: reading, math, and writing. Spelling is considered part of reading and every child with learning problems will have difficulty spelling.

In order for us to be effective in helping LD children, we need to appreciate a few things. First, such children are not unintelligent or uncreative. In fact, a high percentage of LD children are both intelligent and very creative. Leonardo da Vinci and Thomas Edison are examples of intelligent and creative people who had learning disabilities. Second, LD children can be helped if parents and teachers can avoid emotional hysteria and practice effective and helpful measures. Third, LD children are different. They do not learn in the same way or at the same rate as many other children. To some extent, then, they deserve adjustments made in their behalf. The problem, of course, is that teachers who teach large numbers of children and parents with more than one child often find it difficult to adjust enough without sacrificing other children's needs. This means that LD children present a problem to schools and families. Therefore, parents should communicate with school personnel and vice versa.

Because most of us will be parents and some will be teachers, it is useful to become acquainted with the symptoms of learning disabilities. Doing so will enable us to be more informed and perhaps more helpful.

Symptoms of Learning Disabilities

The primary reason it is important to correctly understand children with learning disabilities is to save them from further difficulty presented by uninformed parents and teachers. When children are not able to demonstrate success, many parents and teachers assume incorrectly that they are failing to apply themselves adequately or are malingering in some other way. Children with learning disabilities are different from children who learn normally, but they are not failures until or unless our inadequate understanding and treatment confuses and hurts them.

The following are common symptoms of learning disabled children. Few children will manifest all of them, but all learning disabled children will manifest at least one. Information is taken from *The Learning Disabled Child* (Stevens 1980).

Mixed Dominance - Common

It is normal for children to do more things with one side of the body than the other. Mixed dominance exists when a child eats with the right hand, writes with the right hand, but draws and throws with the left. Some children do not establish cerebral dominance until the age of six or seven. Therefore, if a child manifests mixed dominance after that age, it is likely a symptom of a learning disability.

Directional Confusion - Typical

LD children frequently have difficulty with directions. They may be able to point to the north or south, but cannot find the right word to use at the same time. They may confuse instructions to find something "over there" or to "turn right." In addition, they may be confused about right or left when asked to distinguish between ears, eyes, and hands.

Similar Learning Problems in Other Family Members - Typical

LD children often have parents or other family members who also have learning disabilities. There is no clear evidence that all learning disabilities are inherited, but there is enough to suggest that at least thirty to forty percent of the time other family members will also have disabilities.

Extreme Difficulty with Sequencing - Typical

The learning disabled have a very hard time remembering a series of things in order. At first this may not seem to be too much of a problem, but it usually causes great difficulty. In this case, the child will have difficulty remembering the alphabet, the months of the year, the digits in a phone number, or other numerical sequences.

Slow or Delayed Speech Development - Not Common

Some children are slow to develop in all areas. They may have speech difficulties and sometimes these may be a part of a learning disability. Usually, however, lags in speech development will be corrected with maturation.

Difficulty with Time and Time Relationships - Typical

This may manifest itself as difficulty reading a clock or difficulty following time directions such as, "Be home by five." In addition, children may have difficulty using time to regulate themselves such as bedtimes, times allotted for chores, or mealtimes. Usually a signal has to be given to help a child recognize a certain "time" has arrived. Practically, this may cause little problem because children rely on others for time. But the child may feel "stupid" and feel confirmed in the thought that something is terribly wrong with him or her.

Retrieval Problems - Rare

This usually appears as difficulty finding the "right words." Children with this problem will lose arguments, will not be able to discuss ideas well, and will frequently be misunderstood. They may be able to understand words through reading and listening, but they may have difficulty writing and speaking. They often appear to be lazy, daydreaming, indifferent, or to have a mental block. If you notice that these behaviors are present when children are faced with the task of expressing themselves, then a retrieval problem likely exists.

Poor Motor Control - Common

This is manifest as clumsiness and awkwardness. These children will usually be the last chosen for a ball team and will show poor coordination at other times. They may be able to draw or write well, but will have difficulty in the larger motor tasks.

Problems with Attention, Short Attention Span - Typical

LD children tend to have extremely short attention spans. This means that they will tune in briefly, but will quickly go on to something else. Their attention in demonstrated in short bursts.

Distractibility - Typical

Most LD children are easily distracted. The least little noise or disturbance breaks their concentration. That is why they benefit from small school classes that are tightly structured to keep them on task and be effective in their work.

Hyperactivity - Common

Besides short attention and distractibility, hyperactivity is a common indication of a learning disability. In this case the problem is physical. A hyperactive child cannot sit still, is constantly in motion, is always on the move, and will wander, bounce, and wiggle. Some learning disabled children are hyperactive, but most are not. Further, hyperactivity is not necessarily a learning disorder. So it is important to understand whether hyperactivity is part of a learning disability or not. It is a medical problem that can often be treated with appropriate medicine. However, its treatment should usually involve psychological help.

Tendency toward Reversal - Typical

A learning disabled child will often read letters backwards and sometimes upside down. A child may look at the word "got" and read "pot," "dot," or "bot." Certain letters (m, w, n, u, b, d, p, g, and q) will be reversed more commonly than others. This problem may also show up in math where a child will scramble the order of numbers, such as making a 720 into a 270. All young children make reversals, but most grow out of the problem. LD children do not, and by the age of eight or nine distinctly show a tendency to reverse letters and sequences of numbers.

Poor Oral Reading - Typical

This usually manifests itself as difficulty reading the small words. Some parents and teachers are confused because the same children who can read words like "elephant" and "Mississippi" cannot easily read "who," "from," and "what." They may be intelligent in many other ways, but will have difficulty with oral reading throughout their lives.

Poor Handwriting and Dysgraphia - Common

When first learning to write, LD children have trouble remembering what the different letters look like. Children may know that they need to make a letter "g," but instead make a "y." Few children will manifest all writing problems, but all learning disabled children will manifest at least one.

Inability to Copy - Common

This means that a child will have difficulty copying examples of other written words. This may include copying addresses, phone numbers, dates, and times. It is a frustrating problem.

Poor Spelling - Typical

Difficulty with spelling is the most sensitive indicator of a learning disability. Many LD children conquer their problems in other areas but never manage to become better than adequate spellers. Almost all LD children are poor spellers. This is often caused by difficulty in remembering a sequence of letters and the tendency to make reversals. Also, LD children often do not have good visual memories.

Trouble Getting Ideas onto Paper - Common

Even though children may be good at expressing themselves orally, if there is a learning disability, children may not be able to easily put these thoughts onto paper. They will hate to write and may frequently complain, "I don't know what to write about." Such a child may also explode with frustration when faced with a writing task.

Behavior Problems - Typical

It is frustrating to have a learning disability. Many LD children demonstrate this frustration by disobeying rules in school, at home, and with friends. They may also demonstrate emotional problems such as high anxiety or inability to adapt from one situation to another. These problems may occur because of the learning disability itself or because of late cognitive development and beliefs that they are stupid or otherwise flawed. Usually the lack of traditional success in school and elsewhere motivates them to find a place where they feel accepted and difficult tasks are not required. Unless treated properly, behavior problems can set the stage for future difficulty such as delinquency and criminal behavior.

Creative - Common

Learning disabled children are frequently very creative. This may be manifest by inventiveness or artistic creativity. Leonardo da Vinci and Thomas Edison are two famous examples of creative people who also demonstrated disabilities. ❈

Perception

Learning about the world begins with the processes of sensation and perception. Sensation is the process of having some nerve stimulated, which sends a message to the brain. Sensation is an anatomical function. Most parents will have no influence at all upon how a child senses the world. The only exception to this would be a child who is blind or deaf. In such cases, parents will have to help them receive sensory information. Over ninety-five percent of children are born with sensory equipment that works and they do not need any help to experience the world. Sensation consists of a stimulated nerve sending a message to the brain.

Dozens of impressions are sent to a person's brain every moment of his or her life. There are so many messages that the brain cannot notice all of them. The process of noticing a message that is coming to the brain is called perception. Parents have a great deal to do with helping a child perceive the world. Children do not know which of the many messages that are being sent to their brains they should notice. It is not the case that children innately know which messages are the most important. Someone has to teach them.

Figure 1 will look familiar to you. The line has two sections, A to B and B to C. Look at these and decide which of the two parts of the line is longest. You've seen this many times, so you know that line AB and line BC are the same, even thought they don't look the same. If you saw this for the first time, what would you think? As a matter of fact, since we knew that you have seen this many times, we have purposely made the line so that AB is longer than BC. You can measure it with a ruler if you want to. Illusions like this are tricks that our brain plays on us. Even as adults we don't always perceive things accurately.

FIGURE 1

A third reason for inaccurate perceptions is that our past experiences influence how we interpret things. If three people see the same car wreck, they often give the police three different versions of what happened. The task of parents is to help children perceive the world accurately.

There are five things that a parent can do to help a child perceive the world accurately. First, if children are going to perceive the world accurately, they have to be paying attention to the world around them. A story is told about a farmer who owned a donkey and sold it to his neighbor. In a week the new owner came back to the seller and said, "You have cheated me. This is a very dumb donkey. He won't do a single thing." The original owner then picked up a large board, hit the donkey over the head, and gave the command to "Go!" The donkey started to trot. He then said, "Turn left, turn right," and the donkey obeyed perfectly. The original owner then said to his neighbor, "See? You only have to get his attention."

Parents do not have the option of hitting their children on the head with boards, but they can do many things that will psychologically wake them up so they will pay attention. If a lesson is important for a child to notice, you will want to make the lesson stand out. You can do this in several ways. You can make something stand out from other competing things by making it bigger, brighter, or more colorful. You can do this by having dull things happen before and after the important event. For instance, if we were to teach our children about chastity, we would not do it on a day like Christmas. Christmas is the worst day to try to teach children anything because too many other exciting things are competing for their attention. Pick out a very dull time when you want to teach your most important lessons if you want your children to pay attention.

A second thing you can do to help children perceive accurately is to give them a first-hand experience with the thing you want them to notice. If you want them to learn about a dog, show a real dog. If you want them to learn about airplanes, take them to an airport. This is the value of field trips. It moves children into the real world where all of their senses will be used. They can see and feel and smell the event or object. If you can't give children a first-hand experience, then provide the best second-hand experience available. Your children will probably never stand on the moon. Children are not going to have first-hand experience with the moon, but they can see pictures and photographs taken on the moon by those who were there. They can see rocks that have been gathered and brought back from the moon. Both of these experiences are better than looking at photographs of the moon taken by telescopes. Therefore, give the best second-hand experience that you can.

Third, build in redundancy. Redundancy is a fancy word for repeated exposures to an object or concept. Give children many experiences with the thing that you want them to learn. If you are trying to teach the concept of red, you show them many red things and label them. You hold up a red pencil and say "red," show an apple and say "red," show a red dress and say "red," and show a red book and say "red." The more things that they associate with the sound of the word "red," the easier and faster they will gain a concept of what red is. Adults usually do not like redundancy and don't need it because they have had so many experiences. Nearly everything new relates to something we've already learned. We make mental connections and know a lot about the new experience. A child needs redundancy. If a parent and a child see something new together, the parent, who has a vast background of prior learning, doesn't need to spend a lot of time perceiving the new thing—a child will.

Look at Figure 2. Our written language is redundant. Figure 2 is an English word in which the middle of each letter is missing. You probably will not be able to read it.

FIGURE 2

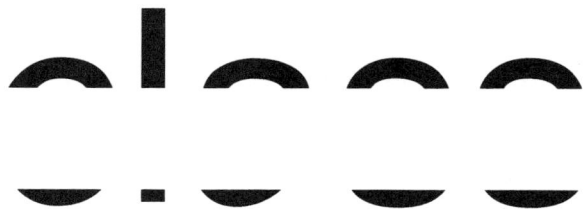

FIGURE 3

Notice that Figure 3 has the same letters, to which were added three small marks. Nearly all adults can read the word. Very few children at age five will be able to read the letters because they have not seen as many English letters as you have. English letters are so redundant to you that your brain fills in the missing parts.

Fourth, to help children perceive accurately, put new experiences into a framework of things they already know. Suppose you are taking a child on a trip and you are passing a goat farm. Take advantage of a teaching moment and say, "Oh, look, out in the field. See the goats?" Your child looks out the car window and, sure enough, out in the field there are a bunch of goats, but there are also some cows, horses, pigs and chickens, tall trees and buildings, and a tractor or two. The thing that catches your child's eye might not be a goat. If he noticed a large tree, he might think that the tree is a goat. It's not enough just to point out something. You need to give the child a frame of reference. It would be nice if you would say,

"Goats are animals that look like large dogs." That's a pretty good description of a goat. Looking into the field, the child will eliminate cows, horses, pigs, chickens, trees, buildings, and tractors. In fact, the only thing that the child could not eliminate would be a large dog or maybe a sheep. When you make use of this principle, you should remember not to be too cute.

Children do not have the same things stored in their minds that you do, and so the frame of reference has to fit the child's understanding, not yours. For instance, the parent in the car looking at the goats could say, "Look at the goat! A goat is a mammal that looks like a miniature, cretinized yak." This is a great description of a goat, but none of the words have any meaning to four year olds, so they wouldn't know what their parent is talking about.

Last, when you teach children something that you want them to store in their brains and be able to retrieve later, you need to give it a distinctive label. Suppose all the animals in the barnyard were called wig, wug, wog, woog, weeg, wag, wague, and so on. The child would be twelve before knowing the difference between a wug and a wog, and a woog and a weeg, and a wag and a wague! We give animals distinctive names such as chicken, pig, cow, and horse, so children can recognize them easily in their minds. The other side of this coin is that children innately think that when things have different names, they are different things.

Contemplate the confusion that arises in a three- or four-year-old child who has been taught that the name for his penis is "dingy," and who has three little friends who have been taught they have a "widdeler," a "tweeter," and a "number one." These children are going to think that they are odd because no one else has what they have. To relieve this anxiety, this little boy may sneak off and play games like "doctor" with his friends just to see how different he is from everyone else. What a relief when he discovers that his friends are all the same or come in two varieties. ❈

Individual
Differences

Most people have at least an intellectual awareness that human beings differ from one another. We can see variations in height, weight, skin color, and other obvious indications that this idea is true. Yet, at the same time we acknowledge we are different from one another, we make general conclusions that certain groups of people are alike. For example, we might think, "All Idahoans or Californians or Chinese or Americans are alike." With some prejudice we might even develop feelings of dislike about some groups of people and treat them with that attitude.

It seems more effective and mature to understand that humans are both similar and different.

More so, however, understanding exactly how we are similar to and different from one another is a major part of all successful relationships.

Parents are likely to be better if they recognize similarities and differences in their children. Then they can adapt what they do based on their knowledge of each child. Employers and supervisors are usually more effective if they understand each person as an individual. Likewise, husbands and wives have better marriages if they are able to communicate. They can recognize unique characteristics in each other as well as communicate what they share in common. As we indicated earlier, all of these are possible if we can select a useful way to determine how human beings are similar and different.

Similarities and Differences in Child Development

First, let's recognize that there will be too many similarities and differences to fully describe. We can, however, select some basis for you to use when you try to understand others. For example, young children demonstrate a set of characteristics called temperament which can be used to recognize both similarities and differences. Thomas and Chess (1970) compared and contrasted children on the basis of: (1) rhythmicity, (2) approach/withdrawal, (3) adaptability, (4) intensity of reaction, (5) quality of mood, and (6) activity level. These six characteristics were used to determine similarities and differences in children.

Thomas and Chess concluded that *easy* children are very regular, have a positive approach to others, are adaptable, have a low or mild reaction level, have positive moods, and demonstrate a variable activity level. *Slow-to-warm-up* children demonstrate varied rhythms, initially withdraw from others, adapt slowly, have mild reactions, have slightly negative moods, and have low to moderate activity levels. *Difficult* children are irregular in their emotional and behavioral rhythms, withdraw from others, adapt slowly, have intense emotional reactions, negative moods, and varied activity levels.

Their scheme helped people understand how to compare infants and recognize similarities and differences. While this method may be very useful for infants, as children mature we might be interested in using additional means to identify similarities and differences. For example, we might want to know about physical characteristics such as coordination, fine motor skills, and size. We might also want to know about cognitive styles such as attentive or distracted, impulsive or reflective tendencies. Social maturity might include inclusion with friends or isolation. We might also compare and contrast children on the basis of emotional behavior such as expressive or inhibited. These characteristics are shown in the table on page 94.

When we are thinking about teenagers, we might use additional ways to find similarities and differences. We might, for example, be interested in early

Physical Abilities	Coordinated	Awkward	Rhythmical
Cognitive Style	Attentive/Distracted	Impulsive	Reflective
Social Maturity	Included	Isolated	Disruptive
Emotional Maturity	Expressive	Inhibited	Volatile
Language Development	Verbal/Nonverbal	Mostly Talks about Objects	Mostly Talks about People
Gender Characteristics	Masculine	Feminine	Mixed

or late physical development and achievement behavior in terms of organization or disorganization. We might consider social behavior in the form of compliance or noncompliance, conversant or withdrawn, active or passive. We might also measure cognitive style, but in different ways than we used earlier. For adolescents, we might be interested in whether thoughts are abstract or concrete, integrated or fragmented.

Understanding and Evaluating

At the same time we are learning about ourselves and others we acquire a system of evaluating what we learn. We start by thinking about it as good or bad, right or wrong. Later we might make comparisons such as better or worse, bigger or smaller. In any event, these evaluations help us make judgments about what we do and how we act. However, many people mistakenly use a system of evaluation on other people before they take time to understand. Black or white skin, tall or short, thin or fat ordinarily are not traits which should be evaluated as good or bad, right or wrong. As part of improving your abilities to recognize similarities and differences in people, it will be useful to develop the skill of gathering information without making judgments.

You can, for instance, learn to suspend judgment until you have had more opportunities to observe someone. In a conversation, for example, you might hear something and commit yourself to ask three more questions about a person's opinion before you allow yourself to evaluate it. You may also avoid evaluating someone when you know you do not have adequate amounts of information about them. Hearing a rumor or watching someone in one situation is usually not enough information to make an evaluation about someone with any degree of accuracy.

Parents often make the mistake of evaluating before they understand. They establish rules which they expect children to comply with. When a child misbehaves, the strain of parenthood often results in impatience shown by instant scolding, spanking, or some other form of punishment. In doing this, parents communicate that the rule is more important than the child. In contrast, suppose parents learned to talk and ask questions until they collected enough information to make a judgment. Then, they may still discipline a child but the child will believe he or she has been understood and the discipline is related to the information given to the parents. In this way, parents communicate their ability to understand similarities and differences, or uniqueness, in each of their children. ❦

The Brain and the Nervous System in Child Development

During the last two decades, neuroscientists have uncovered many hidden secrets about the human brain and nervous system. We now know more answers to many puzzling questions and also know there is much more to learn. The study of the brain and nervous system is at the forefront of science and offers the potential for many exciting discoveries in the years to come.

We are particularly interested in the brain as it pertains to other developmental concerns. We can assume that the brain is involved in everything humans do, but knowing how it is involved and how the brain accomplishes its purposes is essential if we hope to have a more complete understanding of child development.

The Brain's Smallest Unit

Understanding the brain begins with some awareness of a motor neuron, the brain's smallest unit. Millions and millions of these cells are the tissue which forms the structure of the brain and determines how it functions. Each of these cells is made up of a cell body called a soma where the nucleus of the cells exists. The soma is like a message center which receives and sends electrical messages. It receives these messages from many fibers called dendrites. The message passes through the soma to one long fiber called an axon.

An axon is coated by the myelin sheath, a fatty substance which insulates the axon fiber and increases the effectiveness of transmitting the electrical message. We can find some terminals and terminal buttons at the end of the axon. These lie close to dendrites of other nerve cells and form synapses which are connections between neurons. The parts of the neuron can be seen in Diagram 1 on page 100.

The Central and Peripheral Nervous Systems

Cells are organized into clusters and fibers. In every muscle and organ, these nerve cells are organized into two cooperating systems in order to collect information and transmit them to the brain, and from the brain to other parts of the body. The nerve cells of the brain and spinal column make up the central nervous system (CNS). The peripheral nervous system is a collection of nerve fibers lying outside the spinal cord in the skin and other organs of the body.

One part of the peripheral system is known as the autonomic division. It is divided into two parts, the parasympathetic and sympathetic divisions. The parasympathetic and sympathetic divisions are of special interest to us because this is the part of the brain and the nervous system that maintains a steady, or homeostatic, state.

This normal, healthy feeling is maintained when arousal of the sympathetic system is balanced by the energy conserving efforts of the parasympathetic system. If there is great fear, sexual desire, curiosity, or other stimulation, the sympathetic system responds but is balanced by the attempts of the parasympathetic to conserve energy. Both arousal and energy conservation seem automatic because they take place without conscious effort from us. (See Diagram 2 on page 104.)

The Nervous System

To understand the nervous system and its functions, it is helpful to have some knowledge of its most basic units, the nerve cells or neurons. Although neurons vary in size and shape, they have many features in common. Examine Diagram 1 on the following page to understand more about the neuron.

Diagram 1

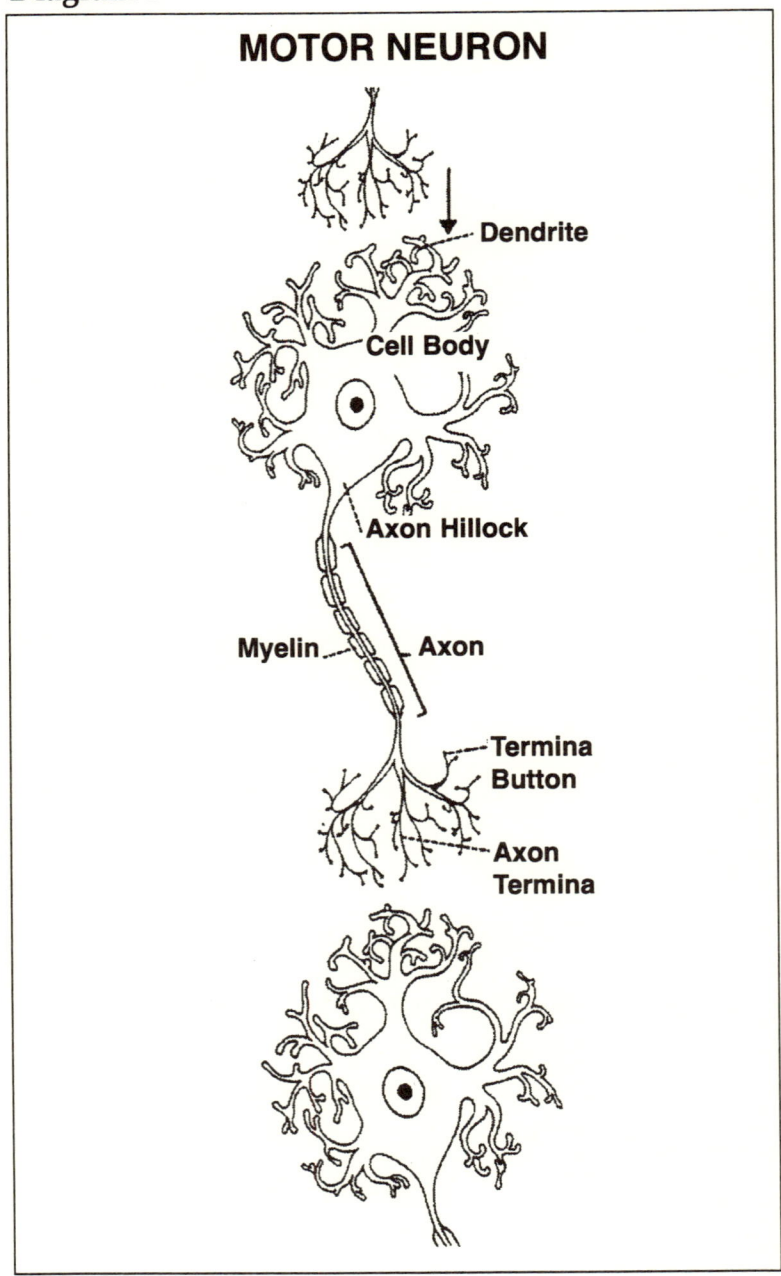

MOTOR NEURON

The Neuron

Axon: the fiber of a nerve cell (neuron) which carries nerve impulses away from the neuron cell body.

Axon hillock: the portion of the neuron where axon and cell body connect.

Axon terminal (also called synapse): the junction between the axon end of one neuron and the dendrite or cell body of another neuron.

Cell body: another term is the soma. It is the portion of a nerve cell which includes a cytoplasmic mass and a nucleus, and from which the nerve fibers extend.

Dendrites: the nerve fiber that transmits impulses toward a neuron cell body.

Myelin: fatty material that forms a sheath-like covering around some neurons. Myelin is important with respect to the speed with which neurons conduct nerve impulses and with respect to the nutritional state of the neurons impulse conduction on myelinated fiber, which is ten to twenty times faster than conduction on unmyelinated fiber.

Terminal button or synaptic knob: tiny enlargement at the end of an axon that secretes a neurotransmitted substance.

The Structure of the Brain

After learning a few ideas about the basic parts of the brain and nervous system, we can now go to reasons why the brain is fascinating. To begin with, our brains have several built-in abilities. That is, the structure of the brain is so organized that certain locations carry out specific assignments and these locations are organized in three levels. The brain stem—consisting of the medulla, pons, midbrain, and diencephalon—performs necessary but simpler tasks than the other, more superior parts of the brain. These tasks include the organization and management of simple and habitual muscle responses.

The medulla contains sensory cells for the throat, neck, and mouth. It also integrates reflex activities such as control of the respiratory and cardiovascular system. The pons contains nerves associated with sensory input and motor outflow to the face. The midbrain controls eye movement and the state of wakefulness of the entire brain. The diencephalon, a paired structure with a thin fluid space between the two parts, called the thalamus, is the major relay and integration center for all sensory systems except the sense of smell.

The cerebellum, located at the base and rear of the brain, is the center which controls the skeletal muscles in the trunk and limbs. All body movement is coordinated at this location. By far, the most interesting part of the brain is the cerebrum or cerebral cortex.

Divided into two hemispheres and located at the top of the brain, this part controls the most complex human thoughts, emotions, and actions. You should understand this is accomplished by how it is organized. (See Diagram 3 on page 105.)

The peripheral nervous system can be subdivided into:

1. The somatic division which carries sensory information to the CNS from the skin and musculature.
AND
2. The autonomic division which includes those fibers that connect the CNS to visceral organs such as the heart, stomach, intestines, and various glands.

The autonomic nervous system is a portion of the nervous system that operates involuntarily, without conscious effort. It has specific functions and subdivisions:

A. Functions of the autonomic nervous system:
    1. Maintain homeostasis (equilibrium in the internal environment of the body).
    2. Regulate heart rate, blood pressure, breathing rate, and body temperature.
    3. Prepare body to meet demands of physical or emotional stress.
B. Divisions of autonomic nervous system:
    1. The sympathetic division is concerned with preparing the body for energy-expending actions.

2. The parasympathetic division tends to counter-balance the function of the sympathetic division by aiding in restoring the body to a resting state following an emergency. (See Diagram 2 below.)

Diagram 2

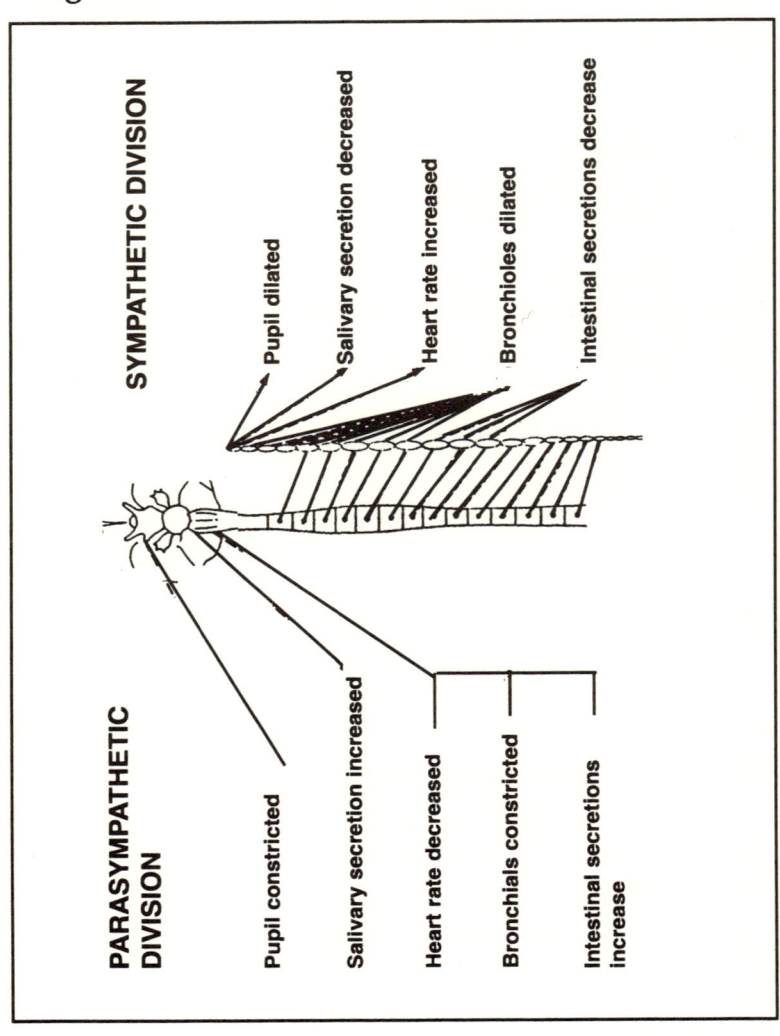

Diagram 3

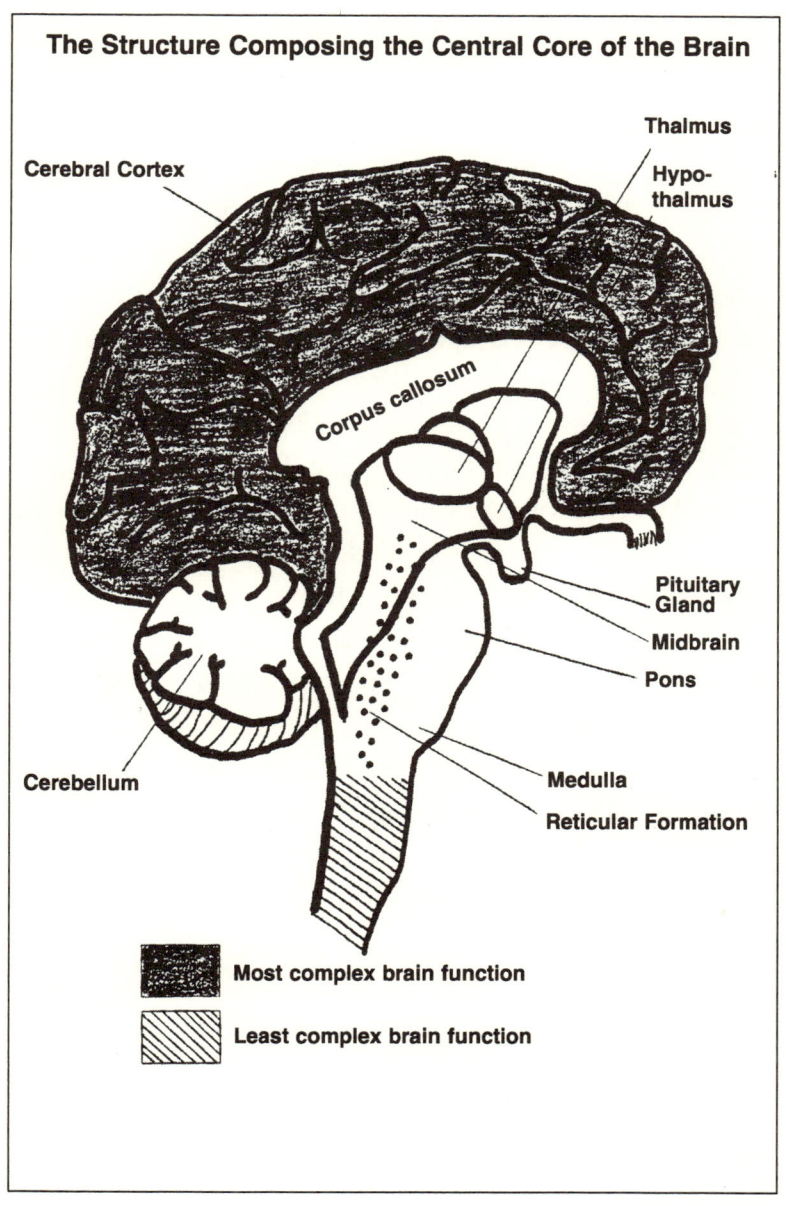

The Structure Composing the Central Core of the Brain

Thalmus

Hypo-
thalmus

Cerebral Cortex

Corpus callosum

Pituitary
Gland

Midbrain

Pons

Cerebellum

Medulla

Reticular Formation

Most complex brain function

Least complex brain function

The Activity of the Brain

First, consider the idea of location. This word has several meanings. It means, for example, that different parts of the cerebrum have specific tasks. In the left hemisphere, the locations for language and abstract thought are located. In the right hemisphere, the locations for understanding spatial relationships, ideational thought such as visual images and simple language functions can be found. (See Diagram 4 on page 109.) In addition to these locations, the cerebrum contains lobes or areas which perform vital, specific, and integrative functions. (See Diagram 5 on page 110.) As you look at Table 1 on page 111, note that each lobe has a function as a sensory area and an association function with the rest of the brain.

In addition to hemispheric and lobe locations, there is another, even more complex function of the cerebrum. Besides the idea of ascending or hierarchical organization, the cerebrum hunts for relationships between ideas. You can, for instance, be working on a problem and decide to think about something else. Your brain will keep working on a solution until one day you may have a pronounced "insight" because your cerebral cortex continued to work on the problem.

Last, in recent years we have heard about being right brained or left brained. This pop psychology suggests that one person can use one hemisphere without the other. Rather, the brain works as an integrated unit. The two hemispheres are connected by a network of nerves known as the corpus callosum. This network enables the brain to communicate and also makes it work as a total unit. It is generally best to think of the brain as one wholly integrated unit.

The Brain and Child Development

Like other forms of development, the brain develops, too. It begins during prenatal development as a cluster of cells on the caudal end of the embryonic disk. From that point on, if growth is unaffected by some teratogenic agent such as alcohol or disease, the brain stem develops followed by the core and cerebellum and lastly the cerebral cortex. During the last trimester of prenatal development there is rapid development of brain cells so that at birth there are thirty to forty percent more brain cells than will actually be used. Most of these eventually die. After birth, brain development takes two forms. One is the creation of innumerable connections between the brain cells and the other is called myelinization. From birth through puberty new connections between neurons are established. This development increases the efficiency of the brain and gives it increased capability.

Myelinization refers to the growth of a fatty insulation surrounding the nerve axon. At birth this is incomplete and increases as an individual matures. This too enables the brain to work more efficiently. Brain physiologists suggest that intelligence or other cognitive skills such as memory are probably a function of the number of connections and how fully myelinized brain cells are. More connections mean more intelligence.

Besides these physical developments, the brain develops according to the amount of stimulation it receives. The brain will respond to stimulation by organizing cell structures to respond. Evidence exists, for example, that mental stimulation enhances natural maturational processes and retards the process of aging. This suggests to us that the wonderfully complex natural brain can be affected to some degree by how we treat it. The more stimulation we provide it, the more it will develop and the slower it will age. What will you choose to do?   ❀

Diagram 4

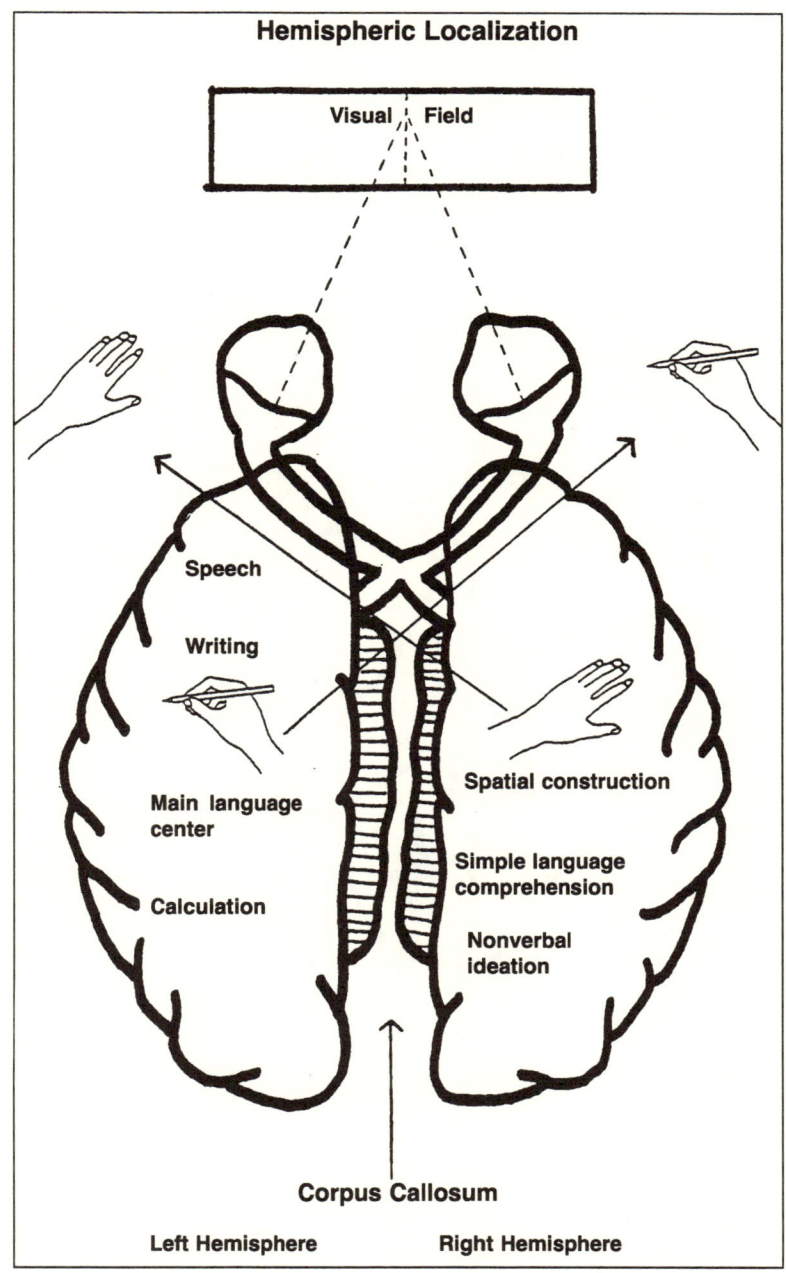

Hemispheric Localization

Visual Field

Speech

Writing

Main language center

Calculation

Spatial construction

Simple language comprehension

Nonverbal ideation

Corpus Callosum

Left Hemisphere   Right Hemisphere

Diagram 5

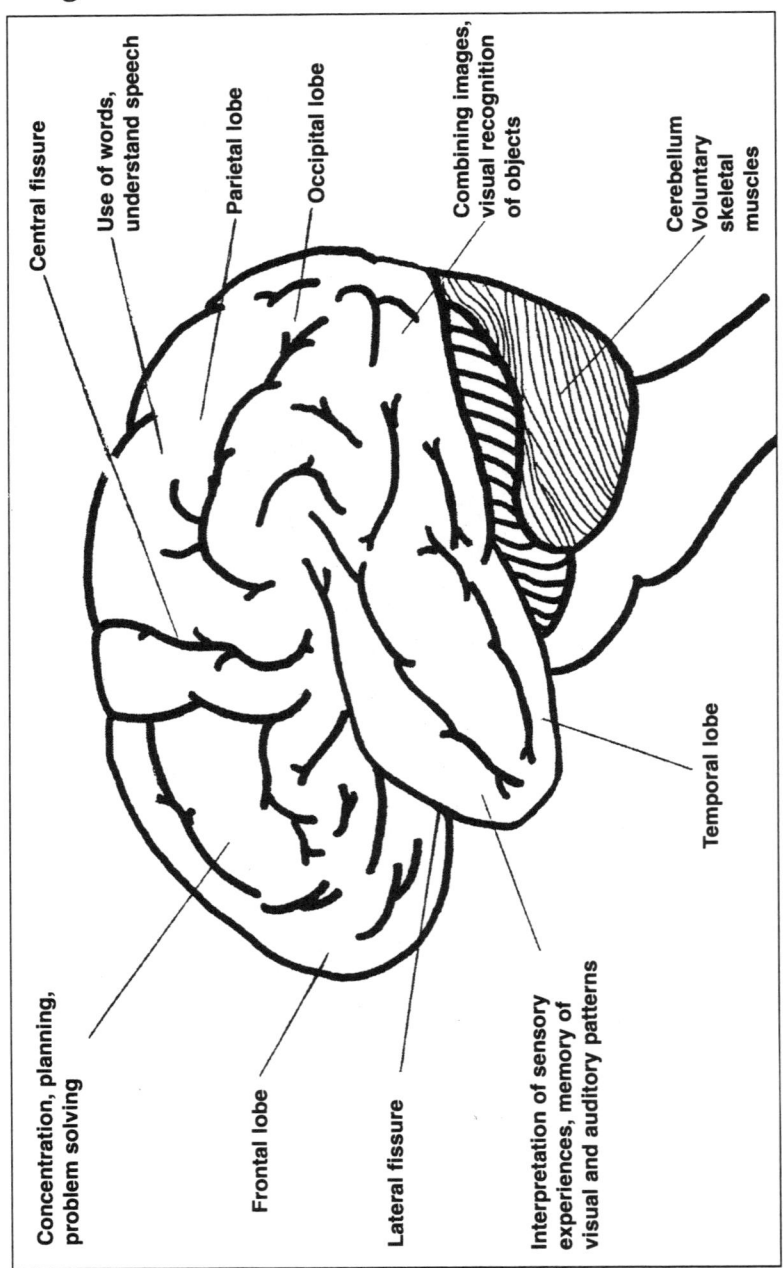

Central fissure

Use of words, understand speech

Parietal lobe

Occipital lobe

Combining images, visual recognition of objects

Cerebellum
Voluntary skeletal muscles

Temporal lobe

Concentration, planning, problem solving

Frontal lobe

Lateral fissure

Interpretation of sensory experiences, memory of visual and auditory patterns

Table 1

Frontal Lobes	Motor areas control movements of voluntary skeletal muscles. Association areas carry on higher intellectual processes such as those required for concentration, planning, complex problem-solving, and judging the consequences of behavior.
Parietal Lobes	Sensory areas are responsible for the sensations of temperature, touch, pressure, and pain from the skin. Association areas function in understanding of speech and in using words to express thoughts and feelings.
Temporal Lobes	Sensory areas are responsible for hearing. Association areas are used in the interpretation of sensory experiences and in the memory of visual scenes, music, and other complex sensory patterns.
Occipital Lobes	Sensory areas are responsible for vision. Association areas function in combining visual images with other sensory perceptions.

Windows of
Learning

E arlier this century, a naturalist by the name of
Konrad Lorenz discovered a biological law
which gave us new understanding and exciting
information about human development. At the time,
most people thought that newborn infants were passive and unresponsive individuals and continued in
this way for several weeks or months. Many believed,
and many still believe, that infants are like "blank
slates," because they inherit very little or bring very
little with them into life when they are born. Lorenz's
discovery was the first to introduce that newborn
infants are very intelligent, highly adaptive, and come

into life prepared with many abilities which enable them to learn and grow.

As a naturalist, he had observed many species of birds and wondered why newly hatched grey-legged geese, without any training, lined up behind their mother and knew how to follow her as they waddled off to the nearest body of water. He found a nest of eggs ready to hatch, removed the mother, and stood close by to observe. As each gosling hatched, it stood up, looked around, and to his delight and surprise, attached itself to him. After all the goslings were hatched they lined up one after another and followed him. He concluded that they had an inherited response to attach, or imprint, to the first thing that moved.

The discovery of imprinting led to research about human attachment between newborns and their caretakers. Researchers subsequently learned that newborn infants have an inherited predisposition to gaze at the human face and move their legs and arms in synchrony with how fast or slow someone speaks to them. They can tell their mother's voice from all other voices as early as three weeks of age. All this is possible because infants come prepared with some inherited abilities and use them to learn about the world or the environment.

Lorenz continued his research and made one further refinement, adding to the great contribution of his earlier discovery of imprinting. He wondered if imprinting took place at a random time, or whether there was a specific critical period, or definite period of time during which it would more likely take place. While watching newborn goslings one day, he learned that if they failed to see something moving and imprint soon after they hatched, they wandered around for a few moments and then began to crouch down in the grass to hide themselves.

After they displayed wariness or fear, Lorenz concluded they would not imprint on their mother or anything else he tried. He decided there was indeed a critical period where certain forms of development were to take place and if they did not occur during this time, the chances were good they would not occur at all. At the time, many were amazed at this discovery because it meant that the development of a living organism was affected by whether certain environmental events took place at the right time. For example, researchers in human development discovered that infants need the attentive and loving nurture of human caretakers. If they do not receive enough attention, they fail to grow.

Lorenz's research could not be wholly applied to humans. Critical periods, or specific times for certain kinds of growth, have been hard to identify with children. Human development resulting from taking advantage of conditions in the environment appears to be possible during any period of a person's life. During research to find critical periods for humans, however, researchers discovered another, equally important biological law which does appear to apply to human development. During the last twenty years we have learned about something called a sensitive period, which means there are certain times when humans are more sensitive to conditions in the environment. Specifically, whenever the body grows rapidly, the person becomes more vulnerable to the environment. That is, a person will learn more quickly from his or her experiences. A familiar example of this idea can be found during the months of prenatal development.

As most know, there are three periods during prenatal development: the first is two weeks long and is called the germinal stage, or period of the ovum. The second goes from six to eight weeks and is called the embryonic period. The third lasts for approximately seven months and is known as the fetal period. The embryonic period begins about two weeks after conception and is the period of time when the head, arms, legs, and organs of the body appear. This is a period of very rapid growth where the body is extremely vulnerable to conditions in the environment. Most problems resulting from chemicals or illness happen during this period. The body of the embryo is extremely sensitive due to rapid growth.

The idea of a sensitive period has lately been applied to learning and development of the brain. In the last ten years, newly developed technology has allowed us to make observations about the brain that were impossible earlier. Magnetic resonance imaging (MRI) scans allow us to observe the brain and how it functions without intruding on it. The results of this research have enormous potential for every parent who wishes to provide the most opportunities for his or her children and promote their healthy and successful development.

How the Brain Develops

To understand how a sensitive period can be used by parents, it will be useful to understand something about the human brain and how it develops. When a healthy infant is born, there are millions of loosely organized brain cells. In addition, parts of these cells, or neurons, are not complete. Brain development and our capacities to learn and think are the results of two forms of growth.

One of these forms of growth takes place when the individual cells become more mature through a process called myelinization. The second form of growth results when individual cells join together in millions of complex connections, or circuits. Researchers have learned that greater mental abilities are associated with more densely connected brain cells. In fact, if an individual cell fails to become connected to others it will die.

Brain development is faster during the early years of life and gradually slows as the child grows older until the rate of growth is based solely on experience and learning after the early twenties. We can still develop mentally, but it depends not so much on physical growth as on our use of our own mental capacities. In the early years, however, brain growth is more rapid because it is growing at the same time as the rest of the body. As a child matures, learns, and grows there are two very powerful forces which drive this development. One is the inherited timing and characteristics built into our genetic code which determine some part of how fast we grow and how fast we will be able to develop different mental abilities. The other motivation for growth is equally powerful. It is phenomenal motivation of the brain cells to organize and represent what we learn. Our ideas and experiences are matched by a cluster of brain cells which represent each experience. In other words, the brain adapts to the conditions in the environment.

In addition to learning how the brain develops and that its rate of development is faster during the early years of life, we have discovered something else of interest. We know now that certain abilities are built into the structure of the brain, and as the brain matures these abilities are shown in greater and improved development. For example, we now know that every person inherits the concepts of numbers, emotions, language, music, time, and space. Very young children understand that things are numbered without anyone teaching them. They have a natural ability to develop speech and display some emotions. These natural abilities develop from a simple form to more complex forms as the brain matures.

The discovery of these inherited abilities has been accompanied by evidence showing the tremendous influence of what we learn from our experiences. Researchers have found that the locations of memories for certain thoughts or emotional experiences are nearly identical for individuals in the same culture who have similar experiences, but differ somewhat between individuals of different cultures. This is quite astonishing. This actually means that the physical structure of the brain, how the cells are connected to each other, is influenced by what we learn. The brain is so adaptive that the cells form connections or circuitry based on the type of experience or stimulation they receive.

This is the basic idea of windows of learning. What we supply to our children, if we do it correctly and at the right time, can influence how their brains develop. They will grow more connections between the brain cells in certain areas which represent specific abilities. If they have more dense circuits of connected brain cells they will have greater abilities as well.

Sensitive Periods and Windows of Learning

A sensitive period exists when rapid physical growth makes us more vulnerable to influence around us. Knowing these sensitive periods can enable us to direct the growth of our children' s brains, accelerate their abilities, and provide an advantage for them. This can be illustrated by understanding a little about the way language development takes place.

A child's inherited abilities can be influenced and improved by his or her experiences. For several years we have known that all infants make the same sounds shortly after birth, but sometime between three and four months of age the child's brain makes a "commitment" to the sounds he or she hears more often. After that, an infant becomes more sensitive or alert to these sounds and, of course, eventually learns to use them to speak and communicate in what is called the "native" language.

At the same time, the infant becomes less sensitive to sounds not heard frequently. This means that at birth an infant is "open" to any language but eventually adapts to the language sounds it hears most often. All this is happening during a sensitive period, a time of phenomenal growth when a child's brain is especially vulnerable to environmental influence. Sounds repeated frequently during this time and heard by the infant will be adapted to by the infant's brain and more easily learned. This is why a child whose parents speak in two languages will have an easier time learning both, and with a better accent, before ten years of age.

We can learn three things from this example. First, we can recognize that children's brains are more vulnerable to influence during sensitive periods, or times of rapid growth. Our ability to exert influence on the structure of the brain gradually declines as the rate of growth slows. Secondly, the physical structure of the brain, connections of brain cells, is influenced by environmental stimulation as a natural part of growing up. By organizing the types of stimulation children experience, it is likely we can influence the structure of their brains and create greater advantage for them. Third, our ability to exert influence on the brain is greater if the stimulation we provide happens during a sensitive period and matches inherited abilities such as language, numbers, and emotions.

Early Brain Development Creates an Advantage

A British anthropologist, Basil Bernstein, conducted an interesting study showing how early brain development increases the possibility of later success. He went to several elementary schools and asked the headmaster to identify the children who had recorded the highest and lowest achievement. Then he went to their homes and asked their parents how they described "school" to their children. He found that some parents used an "expressive code of communication," where they used more words to provide more detailed descriptions of school and what happened there. Other parents used a "restricted code of communication," where they used fewer words and described fewer things about school. They often talked to their children by saying two word sentences such as "Be quiet," "Get off," or "Shut up." He found that children learning in homes where parents used expressive communication were also those with records of the highest achievement. Children whose parents used the restricted code were more likely to be among the lowest performers at school.

At the time of his research, the results suggested that expressive family communication helped children adapt to schools because school teachers used a lot of spoken and written communication as part of instruction. Children who used language better and knew more of it participated more successfully because their abilities matched the situation where good language skills gave them an advantage. Now, we could interpret Bernstein's findings to suggest that the style of family communication actually influenced the structure of children's brains. Those who had a more expressive code of communication had a more elaborate brain structure and could use these abilities when they were required to be successful. Those who grew up around a very restricted code of communication did not have these abilities and had more difficulty succeeding when their school environment required it of them.

The foregoing example illustrates the connection between language abilities and school achievement. Let's consider another example. Like language, children inherit certain basic emotions. Anxiety, or fear, is one of these. Suppose in the early years of life a child experiences much fear, threat, worry, and apprehension. Brain researchers have found that such children build a more dense connection of brain cells in the areas which are designed to create wariness or alertness about things which might threaten them. Suppose after this is accomplished, this child is sitting listening to someone tell a story. One child who has known more security and positive care might be alert to the story and remember it. The other child who has a brain structure designed for alertness or protection may be listening to the story, too, but instead of remembering it, may worry about whether the teacher will hurt him or her in some way. This suggests that early emotional experience can be built into the structure of the brain, the effects of which may last for a lifetime unless altered by some subsequent experience.

This example also demonstrates that early experience, as built into the structure of the brain, can create increased opportunities for later success. Most of us want to know that we are providing the best possible opportunities for our children. The idea of windows of learning affords us one of the greatest opportunities to do so. It is practical and it is positive. It provides a way for us to have lasting positive influence on our children.

Three Windows of Learning: Emotions, Language, and Numbers

As we learn more about windows of learning we will probably find there are several inherited abilities which can be enhanced during sensitive periods of brain growth. At this time, however, there are three which appear to have clear and relevant possibilities for parents. We know how to use them to help promote the success of children. These three inherited abilities are emotions, numbers, and language. By working to provide the right type of stimulation and learning in these areas during periods of rapid brain growth, we can give our children a greater basis for later success.

Imagine some of the possibilities. Emotional abilities are necessary in every social relationship. Understanding several emotions, how to display them, and how to interpret other people are keys to success. Those with greater abilities typically have more successful relationships first at home, then with friends, later on in school, then at work.

Suppose as a parent that you used a window of learning to improve the emotional abilities of your children. That is, you organized a program of stimulation and learning which improved the structure of their brains. Not only would you be taking advantage of a time when your children are more susceptible to learning, but by adding to their early brain growth, you are creating greater possibilities for the rest of their lives.

Children might be less shy than they would otherwise be. They might be more confident and less afraid. They might be more expressive and find it easier to communicate and be understood by others. They might have better impulse control and be able to regulate their emotional behavior instead of getting out of control. They could more accurately understand other people and develop better social strategies. They could more likely trust their emotions in developing friendships, and later on, in marriage and family life. Currently, researchers believe the window of learning for emotions is from birth to age five.

Now, think about the uses for numbers. Doing well in school math is only one. Reasoning about numbers improves the ability to think by using logic and other mental abilities. Numbers are employed in managing money and time. This ability is used in creating organizations of people, setting goals, and developing plans to achieve goals. It is involved in a host of other parts of life. Suppose as a parent you can substantially improve your children's ability to use and reason about numbers. You are not simply teaching them good ideas but actually creating a brain structure which will serve them well throughout their lives. You are increasing the possibilities for success in every situation where numbers are involved. Researchers estimate that the window of learning for numbers is from birth to five years of age.

Lastly, review some of the numerous uses for language abilities. The most familiar are reading, speaking, and writing. Language in society, however, also carries with it our cultural values and the way we think. Our ability to think and reason well is embedded in our language. Developing good brain structure for language also can lead to increased creativity, better use of logic, and more effective problem solving. By improving children's language abilities you also increase the likelihood they will more successfully participate in your culture and accept the values which you believe to be important.

Improved abilities in language will enable children to make a greater contribution to those around them through leadership and other forms of service. If they do not have good language abilities, they are less likely to feel comfortable in taking advantage of these opportunities. The sensitive period for language appears to be from birth to ten years of age.

Taking Advantage of Windows of Learning

The idea of a window of learning implies great opportunity but it also suggests that a time may exist where the possibilities are reduced. We have learned in the last decade that we learn, change, and develop during every period of our lives. Windows of learning simply suggest there are times when the opportunities to promote positive development are greater than at other times. Since these tend to be early in a child's life, these times may also provide lasting possibilities.

Taking advantage of these opportunities is possible if you learn what you can do to provide the right type of influence and stimulation in an effective way at the time when children are more sensitive to it. This will include understanding some things about emotional development, language development, and the development of thinking about numbers. Then, you can learn how to organize your family to provide the most successful and effective learning environment.

Lastly, you can acquire new abilities yourself which will enable you to effectively employ activities designed to promote your children's brain development. It takes place over a long period of time. It is gradual but it is fairly stable once it is done. There is probably no parental activity which provides more

opportunity for you to give something of lasting benefit to your children.   ❀

(This chapter is excerpted from *Windows of Learning*,
by A. Lynn Scoresby, Ph.D.)

Emotions in Children

Our everyday experiences with emotions are so common that we often do not give much thought to the role emotions have in our lives. Even if we recognize their importance, we often do not know what to do about them. You can be a more effective parent if you understand the role emotions have in the lives of developing children.

Knowing the meanings of a few terms will help. Emotional state refers to physiological reactions of the body such as dilated pupils, heart rate, respiration rate, muscle tightening, and so forth. Love, for example, is associated with the heart because muscles close to the heart tighten in correspondence with that emotion. Emotional display, or expression, refers to the many ways we express outwardly what we feel inwardly. Emotions may be expressed or displayed with facial expressions, tone of voice, posture, movement, and language style. Emotional experience is the subjective part of emotion. When you talk about your "feelings" you are disclosing your emotional experience.

How We Acquire Emotions

Researchers are still not certain about whether we inherit some emotions and learn others, or whether we learn them all or inherit them all. At this point in time, however, most are leaning toward the idea that some emotions are built into the structure of the brain. Therefore, some emotions like anger, anxiety, disgust, surprise, and sadness are considered part of everyone's life. Other emotions such as love, for example, may be learned. To further support this idea, researchers point to the finding that fear is not apparent in most infants until about six months of age. For us, however, it is not as important to distinguish between inherited and learned emotions as it is to recognize that emotions are present early in life and play a major role thereafter. We understand that emotions can be learned and children can learn a greater or smaller variety of emotions depending on the opportunities to do so. Further, we can learn more ways to display any emotion if we choose to do that. Lastly, we can, for ourselves and for our children, learn to regulate the intensity of our emotional displays. We can also learn to adapt our emotions to fit into increased numbers of situations.

Emotional Maturity

You might be asking why we should learn more emotions, more ways to express the same emotions, more ways to regulate them, and more ways to adapt them to different circumstances. This process is the pathway to emotional maturity. Children tend to manifest emotions without being aware they do so. They then acquire some awareness that different emotional states and experiences have their own names and accompanying displays. That is, a person can discover anger and then he or she can display anger in certain ways. While this is taking place, children also learn about more emotions, more ways to display them, and also how to regulate and adapt them.

For example, a child can be excited and talkative before going to church, but when in church needs to adapt or change the excitement to reverence. When a child cannot do that, we understand him or her to be less mature than one who can make these adjustments. Further, when children do not know how to regulate their emotional displays, this will be manifest in such behavior as temper tantrums, insecurity, withdrawal, bullying, aggressiveness, whining, and pouting. These characteristics, of course, are usually associated with the less mature.

When parents are faced with immature displays of emotions, they try to help children assume control over their emotions. This may consist of calmly talking children through emotions, giving them the responsibility to gain control by telling them when they are or are not in control. In addition, parents can remove a child from a situation and help him or her regulate and adapt emotions before returning.

Besides the specific techniques of regulating emotions, children learn other management skills. These are developed in part because children mature mentally while they are participating in a family's emotional style. Generally, children learn the same variety of emotions as are expressed in their families. Families who are more expressive will tend to have more expressive children. Families who are inhibited or restrictive will tend to have less expressive children.

When children enter adolescence, they are faced with the need to specialize their emotions, make emotional commitments to values, to other people, and to achievement. During this period, children refine how they display their feelings by making their private feelings the same as their public displays. Sometimes adolescents will be so self-conscious during this period they will, because of security needs, disguise their feelings and mask them with behavior that does not reveal true emotional experience. This condition, though common, limits development toward emotional maturity. When children learn emotional honesty, which means to tell and display outwardly what they feel internally, they will increase their movement toward more mature emotional behavior.

Emotions and Emotional Well-Being

One prominent theory describing how to promote high self-esteem suggests that self-esteem is related to positive emotions. That is, when children feel more love and less fear, more kindness and less anger, more security and less anxiety, they will also develop an overall confidence or trust in themselves. When this condition exists, children demonstrate the characteristics of high self-esteem.

Children will benefit if they are exposed to more positive emotions. As parents or teachers, you may consider the amount of warmth, optimism, happiness, cheerfulness, kindness, and love you express. When children receive these from caring adults, they are more likely to learn how to express them. This will start a cycle which will be repeated, not only in children's lives, but in the next generation as well. ❀

Social Language

Most people are familiar with and accept that geographic and cultural differences affect people's language. In the United States, for example, accent and word pronunciation are used by some to determine where the speaker grew up. Yet, we do not often think about the vocabulary and language style of children as they enter the social world. Social language is an interesting part of child development, and through it one can see the formation of social behavior as children grow older.

Children formulate a language to talk about people, people's actions, games they play, and certain emotional events. Children also create special codes that exclude those who are not well-liked at that moment. They might adopt the style (i.e., accent, vocabulary, idioms) of someone especially admired. Lastly, they create phrases to fit special occasions.

"Ring around the Rosies" and "Eeny Meeny Miny Moe" are examples of game-related sayings. "Geek," "nerd," and "wimp" are descriptions of people. "Bummer" and "yuck" describe emotional reactions, and pig latin is an example of a code children use to speak to each other.

This social language is an important part of childhood society. When children use the same words, the common reference indicates that the speaker belongs or wishes to belong. The most well-known example of this is the vocabulary of adolescent groups. In American society, the actual words change over time, but adolescent vocabulary is constant. Examples include "Valley Girl" language such as "grody to the max" (as bad as possible) and "awesome dude" (great guy).

Other current words are "babe," which describes a pretty young woman, "hunk" which describes a handsome, well-built young man, and the prefix "mega" to describe anything extraordinary. Teenagers who use these words show that they are aware of what other teens know and they display the social cues that evidence membership in groups. Information about social language has mostly come from writers describing the middle childhood years. There is, however, some evidence that children's first words include a social, or interpersonal, vocabulary.

A researcher (Nelson 1973) described a study where mothers recorded the first fifty words of children two years old and younger. The words could be logically classified into two groups. One group described objects; the other consisted of "person" words. One might conclude from this researcher's findings that social language is a part of every child's language development. Further, from early on, children show differences in verbal skills in different situations.

The Importance of Social Language

One important feature of language is the increased freedom it gives us to represent the world without having to show actual objects or act out our thoughts. The development of social language permits children to interact with words and ideas instead of just actions. For example, disagreements can be resolved by talking instead of fighting. Children use language to project a social image and achieve social positions. Children who are hindered in the development of speech and language will also have some difficulty socially.

Social language permits children to form friendship bonds, to be included with other children, and to regulate themselves and others. Those wishing to help children succeed can be expressive toward them as situations are explained, can be conversant with them about their social experiences, and can teach them a social vocabulary that enables children to be aware and sensitive.

Language and Adaptation

Language is social in another sense. It is used, for example, to indicate that a person has recognized the need to make adaptations from one situation to another. We might laugh and speak in louder tones prior to going to church, but when in church our language changes to more reverent tones in order to show we know where we are. Another example of this adaptation is demonstrated in the word selection and voice tones used when one is with a close friend as compared to talking with someone less-known who may have great importance. This adaptation can be found in every language and is called adapting from the familiar to the formal.

Besides changing language to demonstrate adjusting to different situations, language is used to help in making the adaptations. When children are growing up, they discover that language can help them alter their emotions. Suppose, for instance, that a child is overly angry at something which happens in his or her family, or on the way to school. This anger is so great that the child cannot get over it. One of the methods of helping the child change this feeling into another is to use language as a means of making the transition. Language usage in this instance is used to make emotional adaptations.

You can probably imagine how it is important for people to talk through emotional situations. Many, however, are taught something different. Some believe that it is improper to disclose personal information and therefore pretend they are able to avoid revealing anything. Such individuals discover they have more difficulty resolving emotional problems and changing one emotion into another. Generally, those who can disclose about themselves have more success and satisfaction in social relationships.

Sequence of Development

Stage I: Social Vocabulary (Ages 0-3)

Children begin social language by first acquiring a basic vocabulary of people and social-emotional events. During this stage, words are used in simple relationships to the actual event. "I love you," is accompanied by a gesture, for example.

Stage II: Social Rituals (Ages 3-8)

Vocabulary is tied to recurring social rituals. These include games, mealtimes, classroom events, friendship experiences, and shared social events with adults. Children ask questions about social events and begin to use the words of their age group.

Stage III: Social Problem Solving (Ages 8-13)

With an increased vocabulary and awareness, children use words as the means of interacting with one another. They are capable of solving problems and organizing social events. Throughout these activities, social language is used to create such social positions as "leader" and "friend." Language is used and interpreted to reflect an individual's social position compared to other children. First attempts, including using humor in social situations, can be observed.

Stage IV: Social Identity Styles (Ages 13 and older)

Social language is used as a symbol of group membership. Children's vocabulary is expanded to include numerous social situations. Styles of language can be adapted to specific situations (e.g., child and adult, thirteen year old and authority figure, etc). Individuals can be characterized by the style of language they express.   ❁

The Development of Numbers

You probably cannot think of a time when you did not know something about counting or did not use numbers. Recent research suggests there may never have been a time when you did not use numbers. In the last five years, developmental psychologists have discovered that five-month-old infants use and understand numbers. Researchers placed infants in upright chairs so they could see a small screen. They placed a toy behind the screen and, after removing the screen, measured the amount of time the infants watched the toy. Next, they placed two toys behind the screen so both could be seen in the same glance. They timed how long the infants watched the toys. To their surprise, the "watching time" doubled. When they placed three toys behind the screen, the "watching time" tripled. These results suggest that even infants have a primitive form of summing, or adding.

You must think about this ability if you want to organize a program of learning that will enhance your child's ability to use numbers and to develop highly-effective mental structures. Children are especially sensitive to this opportunity from birth until age six or seven. Although they can learn more about numbers and their use in arithmetic or mathematics after this time, they will have passed through much of the sensitive period when the physical structure of their brains can be maximally influenced by exposure to environmental opportunities.

By helping your children develop their use of numbers, you will not only be helping your children succeed in school subjects like arithmetic and mathematics, but you will also be providing opportunities to enhance the quality of their lives in many different situations. We use numbers in managing money, understanding and managing time, organizing and planning, creating, counting, doing arithmetic, using telephones, driving cars, watching television, buying and selling, talking and listening, and more or less in every career choice. Numbers permeate our lives.

It is essential to know how widespread the use of numbers is in life. Understanding how this ability grows and changes over time is equally important because this understanding can help you organize a plan to promote development. You will be able to match what you do with your child's readiness to learn during the sensitive periods along a child's developmental path. Only by understanding this ability can you teach it to your child.

It may surprise you to learn that children's abilities with numbers appear to follow a sequence which starts in a more basic form and develops in an identifiable series of steps. When most of us think about number development in school we think of counting, adding and subtracting, multiplying and dividing, fractions, algebra, geometry, trigonometry, and calculus. As it turns out, these are operations with numbers which can be learned, but they are not the sequence of development. This happens in a different and very fascinating way.

Before describing how this development takes place, there is another point which you can use to be an effective teacher. The idea is that children learn more successfully by concentrating on one or two concepts until they can apply them instead of trying to learn several concepts at once. When you learn about the first stage of development it will be important for you to emphasize and focus on that stage until your child successfully knows it and can apply or demonstrate it in several different situations. This indicates that an easygoing, positive, and consistent effort is better than an intense and rushed approach. Moving on to something else too quickly or trying too much too fast will create confusion and failure rather than confidence and success. Many parts of number development are natural or inherited. This development will happen in some way and in some degree if you only show examples of your use of numbers and expose your child to routine learning opportunities. However, there is evidence that parents can promote learning and add to brain development when they use appropriate methods that match a child's readiness to learn.

Counting

The first step of number development is known as counting. The technical term for counting is "one-to-one correspondence/partitioning and tagging." As you know, counting means to apply a number name to an object or a series of objects and do it in a sequence (one, two, three, and so on). We delight as we watch our children try to count, and when they get it "right," we applaud. On the other hand, when they do not get it "right," we tend to ignore them or make corrections. If, for example, a young child counts "2,3,5, 7," we will suggest that 4 follows 3 and 6 follows 5. This is probably how you were taught, and it is probably how you have been teaching your child.

A closer look will give you some additional understanding about the elements of counting. For instance, we count because we want information about individual things such as how many toys we have, or how many times some repeated thing happens. The need for this information is quite substantial because it helps children understand the world and helps them adapt to it. Counting is one very important way of learning about and organizing information about the world. You might give your child a small ball which is made up of several different textures. Some parts are soft and fuzzy, some are slick, and some parts are made up of stiff hairs. The child learns about different textures as he or she touches the different parts of the ball. Children use touch to learn. In the same way, counting is a method of learning about one or more things such as people or objects.

In order to count successfully, one number must be applied to one object, event, or person. This is called tagging. Tagging is the ability to link a number name to a thing or a series of things. It is very similar to giv-ing the name "Daddy" to a child's father, or "Mom" to a child's mother. However, in this case, the name is a number. Suppose a child sees several toys in front of him on the carpet where he is playing. One of the most common questions asked of him or which he may ask himself is, "How many are there?" Now, in order to answer that question, a child needs to have a number-ing system and be able to apply it to the objects one at a time.

The idea of numbering is inherited, so a child will look at all the objects and sense that some method should be used to learn about them. Counting emerges when parents use the words of their language, point to one object at a time, and give each a number name in a precise sequence. The spoken word and pointing happens in a sequence of tagging each object. This is one-to-one correspondence.

Besides tagging, one-to-one correspondence involves a child knowing the difference between what has been counted and what has not. This is called partitioning. Partitioning means that a child has the ability to classify things or people into two categories: what has been counted and what is yet to be counted. If a child has a total of five toys and has counted three, there are two remaining to be counted. An interesting question is how a child knows this. Again, the ability to classify appears to be inherited and this ability can be significantly enhanced through training and experience.

Before moving to the next stage of development, let's consider why counting is important and why you should be interested in promoting it. First we should note that counting is a way of improving a child's ability to make judgments about things. There are numerous situations where counting is part of what we use to make judgments about things, people, and events. Second, counting is the beginning of understanding important ideas like the concepts of equal and unequal. Suppose an object has a name assigned to it like a "1," and another object has another name assigned to it, such as a "2." The names of numbers make each object equivalent or equal. There is one "1" and there is also one "2." When children learn how to count, they can improve their abilities to understand many other important ideas.

You can watch your child learn to count in addition to acquiring other abilities by doing three simple things. Practice having your child point to an object while saying the number name. This will improve physical coordination as well as accelerate the development of counting. In addition you can ask your child to count out loud. Children tend to do this anyway when confronted with a difficult counting task, but asking them to count aloud will enable you to see if they are tagging and partitioning successfully. When they are, you can praise them, and when they are not, you can show them a better method. Lastly, it is useful to involve more body parts in the counting process. Several years ago, educators thought counting on our fingers slowed it down and restricted other forms of mental development. Now, we better appreciate that counting is accelerated if we use fingers, toes, jump up and down, change voice tones, and make gestures which match the tagging process. The more things we incorporate into counting the more fun it is and the better children learn.

The Stable Order Principle

The next stage of development is called the stable order principle. To understand it, stop reading for a brief moment and count to ten. What you did was use a repeatable set of words in a specific order. Nine always follows eight and precedes ten. Three always follows two and precedes four. The specific order of words is accompanied by another part of this principle.

This is the idea that there is a specific order of words which can be applied to everything being counted regardless of how many there are. If there are five or five hundred objects, for instance, there is a set of number names which will be applied in a repeatable and unvarying order.

Successful development in this stage requires the true combination of what is inherited and what is learned. The idea of counting and numbering is inherited so children will demonstrate this with little or no encouragement. The specific words and the sequence of using the words, however, is learned, and children will not develop in this area unless their environment provides opportunities. Children naturally count things in sequences. This may be 2,3,6, and 7. It may be 27, 33, and 44. Regardless of whether it is correct, the sequence demonstrates that it is a natural ability. Getting the sequence to be correct and unvarying, however, is where learning is required. Usually, as suggested earlier, parents do this in two ways. One is to demonstrate the proper order, and the other is to correct children when they count incorrectly. There are additional ideas for teaching correct order that will enhance your efforts.

It is easier to help children learn by starting with shorter rather than longer lists of numbers. Instead of counting to ten, which is the most common, start with a list of one through five. When children have mastered this, then move on to a list which includes one through ten, and so on. It is also useful to allow children to develop their own individualized way of counting, at least in the beginning. Researchers have found that children two years or older who use unconventional or individualized methods of counting are better able to apply the stable order principle than two year olds who are required to use something imposed on them by their parents.

The researchers who described this idea suggested that imposing an external method of organizing a sequence of numbers interferes with a child's own method. Remember, however, that this applies to children around the age of two who are demonstrating their first attempts at counting in a sequence. It does not apply to children who have counted in sequence for a long period of time and tend to repeat the same errors. In this case, these children are likely having difficulty creating their own sequence and may benefit from understanding one supplied by their parents. In either case, if parents continue to demonstrate a correct counting sequence, children will emerge with the correct sequence faster and more effectively. Lastly, you can help your children learn more effectively by providing creative ways of counting.

The stable order principle suggests that counting in sequence be accompanied by some form of idea about "that's all there is." The idea of completeness helps children know both when counting is not complete and when it is finished and includes all the available objects, events, or people to be counted. Successful development in this stage includes counting in a sequence and understanding that the counting sequence includes everything. This means that numbers are now being used to organize things in a sequence and to organize all the separate things available to be counted.

The Cardinal Principle

The third stage of development follows the first two logically and appropriately. In the first stage, children learn to apply one number to one thing, and in the second stage, they demonstrate the ability to do this in a sequence that continues until all are counted. In stage three, a child develops the ability to make a summary conclusion about all the things he or she has counted. This is often so easy for us that we forget how challenging it is for beginners. This summary conclusion is the last number in the counting sequence because it represents the total number of things counted.

The cardinal principle of numbers is that the last number in the sequence represents a total which is greater than any preceding number and represents everything, or the total number of things to be counted. In answer to the question, "How many are there?" a child will count each separate object, and after applying a number name to each in sequence, will conclude that the last number is the same as the total number of objects. Suppose a child has five little dolls in front of her. Ask her, "How many are there?" She will answer your question by starting with the first one, hopefully pointing to it, and saying "one," then "two," and so on, until reaching the last object and the number, "five." She will turn to you and answer your question by saying, "There are five dolls." She has applied the cardinal principle of numbers.

We are not certain how a child knows that the last number in a sequence represents something larger than the other numbers. Perhaps they know this because of practice counting, but many researchers think that children's brains develop and this knowledge accompanies new and more mature thought processes. If so, it is a truly remarkable bit of evidence about the inherited ability humans have for numbers.

Conservation

Conservation may be a term that is new to you, but it is not new to anyone who studies mental growth in children. Conservation is about children's abilities to make judgments about quantities and qualities. Suppose, for instance, you place two round balls of modeling clay in front of a child. They are the same size. Now mash one and make it flat and much wider than the other. Ask this child, "Which one is larger?" If the child can perform conservation, he will recognize that even though the physical shape of one ball has changed, the amount of clay which makes up the ball has not. Therefore, the child will answer, "They are the same."

When applied to numbers, conservation means that children recognize that two groups of numbers may be the same even though they are arranged, shaped, or colored differently. One group of five purple turtles is the same as another group of five blue stars.

The ability to conserve means that children are recognizing numbers as one way of making judgments about things in addition to color, shape, and size. It is an important step in development because it tells us that children can recognize the constancy of numbers, which is the earliest basis for math operations. Arithmetic students, for instance, will recognize how this is incorporated into learning in the form of sets or groups of numbers. We may know that three feet, for instance, is the same as thirty-six inches but we cannot add these numbers without changing one into the same form as the other. This is possible only because of the ability to conserve.

Later on you can read about methods of promoting development by teaching children about grouping, classifying, or categorizing. For now, one example might illustrate the idea. Many children have been reared watching Big Bird, Ernie, Oscar the Grouch, and Bert. These famous puppets of *Sesame Street* teach children to sing a little song called, "Which of these things belong together?" In this activity, children improve their abilities to group and categorize. When this happens, they are learning to conserve.

Order and Sequence Irrelevance

After children learn to group or categorize to conserve, they demonstrate the ability to recognize that the order or sequence in which things are placed makes no difference to the actual amount of things to count. If, for instance, you had ten small boxes in a row from small to large, there are still ten boxes even if you place them in a row from large to small or place them randomly. This ability is important for several reasons. Counting with numbers is not the same thing as naming objects. If a child counted five toys, she might start with the truck as number one and end with the doll as number five. The next time these five toys are counted, the child might start with the doll as number one and the truck as number five. This ability means that the child has learned that numbers are not fixed like names to objects and are transferrable. That is, a child can use a different number for each object each time they are counted. Numbers are not linked specifically to any object even though they tell us something about the object. This ability is one of the first signs of children using numbers to think abstract-ly, or to think about some mental representation of physical objects. This ability is necessary in order for children to move to the next stage of numbers devel-opment called symbolic operations.

Symbolic Operations

By this time, children have learned to count and to use numbers as one way of thinking about things, people, and events. They have a fairly good ability to place numbers into groups and to make categories of numbered objects. This gives them the ability to use symbols in order to perform different operations with numbers. This is very easy to understand. After children learn counting and have developed through the preceding stages, they are able to do things with the numbers. These are called operations. Addition, for instance, is an operation which sums or combines two or more numbers. It is represented by a symbol, "+," the plus sign. The symbol represents the operation of the activity of adding.

From this point on, children can learn about and develop improved abilities to learn operations represented by new symbols and then apply them to find answers. Subtraction, multiplication, and division follow. Decimals and fractions are different ways of symbolizing parts of numbers. They use the same mental ability.

Using symbols helps children think faster and use numbers in more efficient ways to think about the world. They represent how to use numbers for specific purposes such as adding or subtracting money. From this point, children's abilities with numbers tend to increase rapidly until they master one symbolic language after another. Eventually, these languages include geometry, algebra, trigonometry, and calculus. Each is a way of representing how numbers apply to the way we think about the world in which we live.

We should conclude that helping children develop their abilities in numbers creates much more benefit than simply improved abilities in school math. Numbers are an important part of thinking and reasoning in the world. When children reason effectively with numbers, they are more likely to reason and think more effectively when making a variety of judgments about objects and events. Helping them develop, therefore, is the means of offering enhanced opportunities for their success in a variety of situations. ❀

(This chapter is excerpted from *Windows of Learning: Numbers*, by A. Lynn Scoresby, Ph.D.)

Moral Conduct

It is easier to teach children to think about something than to help them know what to do, when to do it, and how it can or should be done. When it comes to morality, for instance, we typically want them to do what is moral and not just think about it. As teachers, parents, and caretakers we are in positions to help children learn to do what is moral if we are aware and skillful in what we do.

First, we need a definition of morality that makes sense, is easy to teach, and will have power to affect children. Morality is simply intentions or actions which help someone and immorality is intentions or actions which harm someone. Unfortunately, we often fail to teach children what helps or hurts people because we mistakenly think morality is related to conformity to rules. Those who have this notion assume that a child who complies with a rule or law is moral. This is true only if the law and obedience to it helps rather than harms human beings. Instead of thinking that morality is the same as conformity or obedience, we need to teach ourselves and our children what helps and hurts people.

Coincidentally, teaching children about helping or hurting people is one of the most effective ways to ensure they will act morally when a moral decision confronts them. Think about a high school student who has had difficulty with a math teacher. This teacher is generally so disliked that many students have negative feelings. One day, this boy is with a group of friends in the school parking lot. They notice the teacher's car and someone suggests letting the air out of the tires. Another says, "Yeah, let's do it," as he moves closer to the car. Our friend is now faced with a moral dilemma. Should he let the air out of the teacher's tires or not? What will influence what he does? Suppose he says, "I don't know guys. We would be breaking a rule." Would that be persuasive to the other guys? They might think, "What rule?" or "The rule is stupid." Contrast that with the idea that letting the air out of someone's tires would be harmful to him. If the boy thinks about that, then he also might be able to put himself into the situation of someone who comes out of school to drive home and discovers that the air is out of all four tires. Would that line of reasoning be more persuasive? Generally, the answer is that thinking about what helps or harms people is more directly related to moral behavior than pressure to comply with rules.

What does this have to do with getting children to do, not just think about, the moral thing? It focuses them on what they are to actually do. They are to help and not hurt themselves and other people. In addition, when we think about morality in this way it directs us to what we must do as teachers, parents, and caretakers in order to get children to act morally. Notice how children who act morally differ from those who do not.

Children who act morally are more likely to have empathy for others, meaning they understand what others may think or feel. In contrast, children at higher risk for immoral behavior are defensive, which means they are more likely to shift the responsibility for their actions to others and be unable to know about and discuss their own feelings. They do not know what others feel because they do not know their own feelings. Moral children tend to be more accepting of others or willing to understand other people without making premature judgments about them. Prejudice, judging people without gathering individual information about them, is often a characteristic of people who do immoral things.

One interesting condition which relates to whether children do moral or immoral acts is the amount of conversation they have with adults such as parents and teachers. If they participate more frequently in conversation relationships and are less isolated from others, they are more likely to make moral choices and act morally.

The following lists are characteristics of those who are likely to do moral and immoral acts.

Moral	*vs.*	**Immoral**
Empathy		Defensiveness
Acceptance		Prejudice
Autonomy		Vulnerability
Social Interaction		Social Isolation
Activity		Passivity
Positive Moods		Negative Moods

A Teaching Plan

In light of the foregoing it is clear to us that we can influence children by helping them develop some character traits which they express in many different situations. In addition, there are some specific things we can do to ensure that children will do what is moral when they are faced with pressure to do otherwise.

Repetition

This means that our focus on moral traits must be repeated so that children learn they are important to develop.

Rule-Governed Behavior

Children understand that rules exist for most situations. We can help them identify the rules for friendship, social activities, church, meal time, etc. However, we must also teach that rules or laws can help and harm people.

Internalize

After children learn intellectually about helping and harming people, they must actually practice these traits and discuss them so they can test the ideas against their own experience. Later when they more clearly understand they are free to choose themselves. They will internalize these experiences, they will be moral people rather than merely thinking about doing what is correct.   ❀

Friendship

Friends are an important source of influence on developing children. It is by association with friends that children are motivated to learn social skills, and friends give social reinforcement that provides emotional satisfaction. Friendship has received much attention from many writers. One wrote:

A blessed thing it is for any man or woman to have a friend; one human should whom we can trust utterly; who knows the best and the worst of us, and who loves us in spite of all our faults; who will speak the honest truth to us, while the world flatters us to our face, and laughs behind our back; who will give us counsel and reproof in the day of prosperity and self-conceit; but who, again, will comfort

and encourage us in the day of difficulty and sorrow, when the world leaves us alone to fight our battle even as we can.
— ***Charles Kingsley***

Developmental psychologists have learned that children notice and are affected by other children from the time they are infants. Vandell, Wilson, and Buchanan (1980) reported that pairs of children aged six months, nine months, and one year smiled, touched, and babbled to each other. When babies had no toys, they spent more time interacting.

As children develop, their behavior becomes more elaborate, involving new social skills. Observations of preschoolers show that children who smiled and were friendly received more pleasant responses than children who pushed, shoved, or were mean in other ways. This suggests that children engage in reciprocal behavior at an age earlier than researchers thought possible. The children, however, were not aware they were doing so.

In later childhood, friendship develops into more elaborate forms of reciprocal behavior. They view sharing with each other as a sign of friendship and learn ways to give and receive. Some of these ways include exchanging material goods, giving compliments, showing patience with and acceptance of each other's mistakes, and helping each other with chores or work.

Eventually, friendship develops into a significant emotional bond where children share feelings and understand personality traits of one another. Adolescents select friends based on companionship, experience, and similarity of interests. From Leitner's study, we might conclude that children naturally tend to be social and be friends with each other. Social isolation, therefore, must be the result of unfavorable social experience. Further, not having a friend or not having the skills to be one may interfere with the normal course of development.

Children will learn friendship behavior both as part of maturation and social learning. The biological aspect can be helped when children see positive friendship behavior and when they have social opportunities themselves. Such social experience can be frequent and it can be varied. Parents often worry if their children have friends who are older or much younger. The evidence seems to suggest that conditions will not be destructive as long as the friendships are positive and have some meaning for children. The situation creating the most difficulty, of course, is the absence of siblings, friends, or other good friendship experiences.

Sequence of Development

Stage I: Momentary Playmateship (Ages 0-3)

Before the age of four, children choose friends on the basis of physical attributes or neat toys. Friendships last as long as children are curious and stimulated by the novelty or prestige of their friend's characteristic or possession.

Stage II: One-Way Assistance (Ages 4-9)

Children enter this stage of friendship at the time they understand the intentions of other children's actions. Children are still selfishly interested in getting what they want from their friends.

Stage III: Two-Way Fair Cooperation (Ages 6-12)

There is considerable overlap between Stage 2 and Stage 3. As children move into Stage 3, their friendship styles change. They recognize that friendships require give and take, but in a way to satisfy self-interests. True concern for their mutual interests is not yet evident.

Stage IV: Mutually-Intimate Shared Friendships (Ages 9-15)

Children form valued friendships. They are often exclusive, with children feeling quite possessive about them. Cliques of friends often form, excluding those not in the group. Emphasis is on loyalty to one another and mutual help giving.

Stage V: Autonomous Interdependence (Ages 13 and older)

Friendships have a deep emotional commitment. Children can understand the dependence on others and the need for autonomy. Concepts like trust and risking caring for another are relevant. These friendships can last a lifetime. ✿

Why Children Do What They Do

You may not understand why your children act a certain way, but there are reasons. It is important to understand these different reasons. You can be more successful with children if your approach toward them is consistent with the reason for their actions.

One set of parents had a son who frequently wet his pants, even though he was six years old. They tried to be patient, but eventually they gave in to shaming, spanking, or grounding him. Nothing seemed to work. Seeking help from a counselor, they were asked to subject the child to a physical examination. Results showed that the child had a very small bladder. So small, in fact, that he could not retain urine for any appreciable amount of time. Had the parents known the reason for the behavior, they could have been more successful and would not have treated their child destructively.

Behavior Due To a Stage of Development

Behavior may be attributed to a stage of development. Certain cues help identify behavior caused by a developmental stage. First, if you can remember behaving similarly at that stage of your own life, you can be sure that your child's behavior isn't peculiar. It might really be behavior that is prompted by a stage of growth common to all children.

A second cue is if you have seen the same behavior in other children of the same age. A scoutmaster who was having problems with rowdiness with his twelve- and thirteen-year-old scouts came home from a scout meeting and told his wife, "I just don't understand these boys. And the funny thing is the boys I had last year were the same. And the scouts I had five years ago were doing the same things." This scoutmaster should probably attribute the rowdiness to a stage of growth. But, if you're going to use this cue, you need to have seen a lot of behavior. You can be confused by thinking, "OK, I saw such-and-such once, so I know that's what all children are like." Imagine, for example, a student teacher who goes to a room where the full-time teacher is like a dictator. The students come in, sit at their desks, place their hands on top of the desk, and sit looking straight ahead. They do not chew gum, talk to their neighbors, or leave their seats until the bell rings. The children, because they are frightened of their teacher, are models of good behavior. The student teacher might come back from the experience of a week and say, "Boy, eighth graders are at the greatest age in the world! I can't believe how well-mannered, polite, and quiet they are." If so, this student teacher has made two mistakes.

First, the student teacher has not observed enough eighth graders to make valid judgment about what all of them are like. Most eighth-grade children are much more active; in fact, they are at one of the most difficult ages for growing children because they are pushing limits and trying to tell the world that they are not children any more. Second, the student teacher had never observed the behavior of those same eighth graders under less restricted conditions. Children who are coerced, who live in fear, or who have a poor environment probably will not act like children who live in normal conditions.

Recognizing the third cue requires that you become knowledgeable about child behavior. Taking courses in child development and reading about what is expected in normal children helps you establish norms and helps you know what kinds of behavior you can expect from your children at certain ages.

The fourth cue is that the behavior may simply feel right to you. You may not remember it in your own life and might not have seen it happen or read about it, but instinct tells you that the behavior is appropriate for the child's age.

When behavior is caused by a stage of growth, it looks like one of the curves on the graph on page 166. The behavior could start out hardly ever occurring, reach a peak, and then drop back to nothing. Sometimes a child is in a stage for a short time; sometimes for a long time.

Sometimes several stages develop. Consequently, when you have decided that your child's behavior is caused by a stage of growth, you should not blame yourself for it. You didn't cause it; the cause lies within the child. The best thing you can do is to wait the behavior out until growth changes it. Be patient and know that the behavior won't last forever. It will be there for a while and then it will go away. And know, too, that other parents are experiencing the same thing or something very similar with their own children.

Although children sometimes pass through good stages, parents are often unaware of them, attending instead only to those stages that they think are negative. Many times parents aren't even aware that their child is going through a "good" stage.

In other words, the best cure for disturbing behavior that is caused by a stage of growth is to relax. If you can't relax, then try to channel the child into some other behavior that you can stand. If you do stop a particular behavior, you ought to make it clear that you are stopping it because of factors within you. If an action is a result of a developmental stage, the child is not bad; it is just that you cannot let your child act that way. If the action is a result of a stage of growth, try to be patient. The behavior will change by itself.

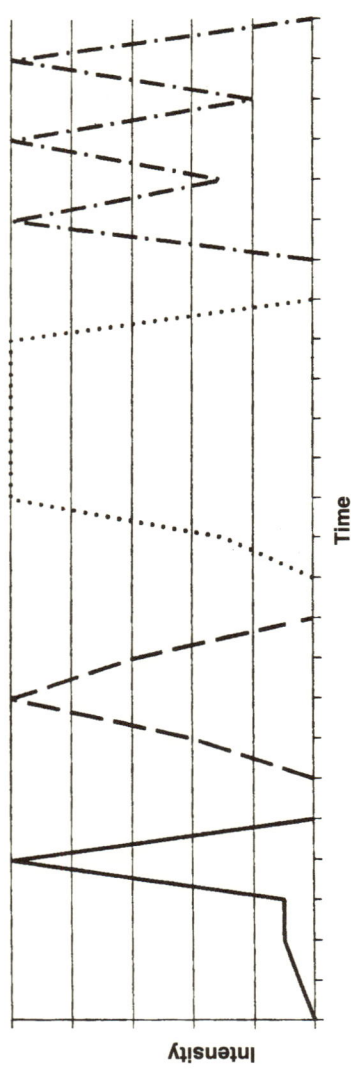

Unfulfilled Needs

Unfulfilled needs are a second cause of behavior. When children's needs are not fulfilled, an internal mechanism pushes them to seek fulfillment and engage in attention seeking behavior. This is a plea from children for someone to help them fill their needs. If their needs continue to not be met, the children's disturbing behavior will accelerate and look like the following:

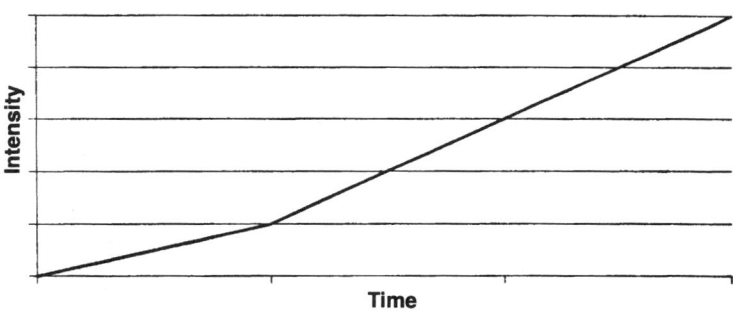

Notice that the disturbing behavior increases dramatically as time goes on. Behavior caused by an unfulfilled need will not go away on its own. It will only get worse. A list of the most important needs of children is found in the chapter "Innate Needs."

Just as there are cues for behavior caused by stages of growth, so there are cues for behavior caused by a desire to fulfill needs. The first cue, and possibly the most important, is that the behavior seems inappropriate for the age of the child. A nine-year-old child who is dragging a teddy bear around is an example of this. The child is, in essence, waving a red flag, saying, "Help! I need some kind of nourishment."

Second, the child's behavior has an electric, supercharged quality to it. You may have known some children who were so tense and anxious that whenever you touched them, you expected an electric shock. Unless they have physical problems, children who are overly active, who run or jump excessively, or who are unable to concentrate may be struggling to fulfill a need.

A third cue of unfulfilled needs is when the behavior doesn't occur in just one situation. The behavior manifests itself at home, at school, at church, and at play. Children try to satisfy their needs everywhere.

A fourth cue is when bad behaviors keep popping up. Even though you may be able to train the child to discontinue one behavior, another behavior will take its place if the basic need is still there. In much the same way, when a person has an infection that manifests itself as a boil on his neck, he can put salve on the boil and clear it up, but another one may appear on his knee. And when he clears that one up, it breaks out again on his elbow, and so on, until the infection, the cause of the boil, is removed. Similarly, when there is an unfulfilled need inside prompting bad behavior, the behavior will not go away until the need is fulfilled. When the cues indicate an unfulfilled need, you must ask yourself, "What's my child trying to tell me?" "What isn't my child getting out of life?" And when you have the answer, you must then satisfy this need.

The cure for behavior caused by an unfulfilled need is, obviously, to fill the need. When parents start to do this, they may see no improvement in their child's behavior for quite a while. Children often test their parents to see if they are sincere in their behavior. Once children are convinced that their needs are going to be taken care of, their undesirable behavior drops off dramatically (as shown below).

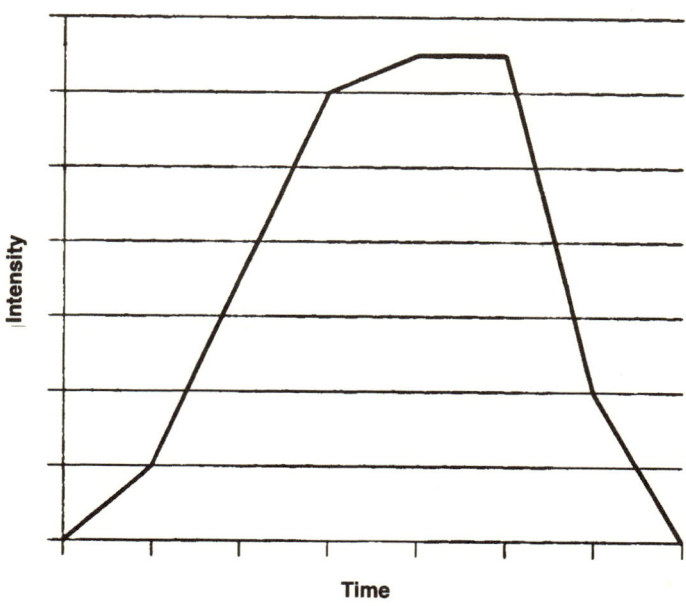

Intensity

Time

A Child's Environment

The third cause of undesirable behavior is some cue or event in the child's environment. If a child begins acting strangely and if none of the above cues explain the behavior, you may need to examine the present environment of your child. Who is present? How are they acting? Or ask yourself if anything traumatic has happened. Did the child move into a new school? Did a parent die? Was there a divorce? Did the child lose a best friend, or was there a fight with somebody at school? If you can pinpoint a dramatic thing that happened at about the time that the child's behavior suddenly changed, you've probably found the cause. This behavior looks like the chart below.

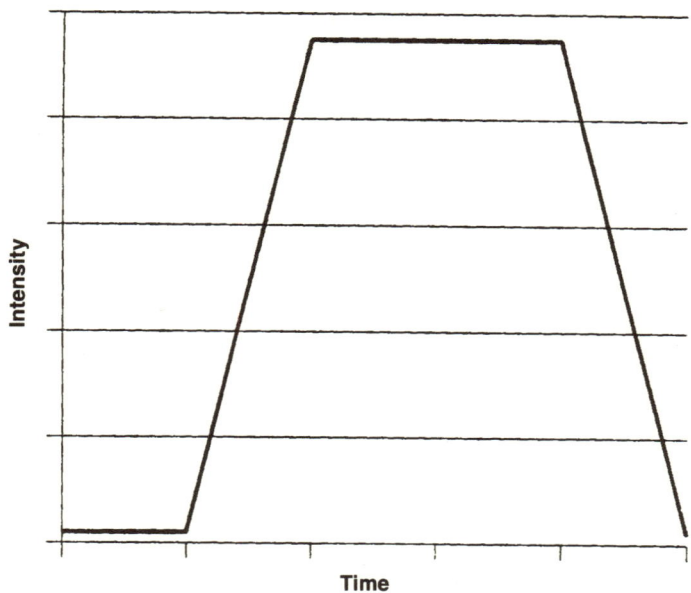

Time

In this case, a child didn't cause the situation; outside forces probably did. And so, instead of growling, "That's a dumb way to behave," a better approach is to be a forerunner for your child to sweep the stones and the stumbling blocks out of the way. If there is trouble with somebody at school, go and be your child's advocate. Learn about the situation and then communicate your support to your child. Maybe it means that you will need to change. But one thing to be careful about is to not allow a child to be irresponsible. If your child brought about something in the environment, he or she must learn to pay the consequence.

The cure for disturbing behavior is to first try to undo the traumatic event. A child who has been transferred from one homeroom to another could be transferred back again. But you can't undo a death or a divorce, and so the second cure is to try to cope with the situation by listening, helping your child understand what has happened, and helping your child work out a plan to solve the problem. When this is successful, bad behavior stops immediately. It looks like a miracle.

A Lack of Knowledge: Ignorance

The fourth cause of undesirable behavior is simply that the child doesn't know any better. There are two reasons for this. First, in families with many children, parents can lose track of which lessons they've taught which child. As a result, they may have forgotten to teach a child a particular lesson. If none of the other listed causes seem to account for the child's behavior, you might decide, "Maybe I'm to blame for this because I didn't teach my child." If you are to blame, don't nag. Sit down and teach your child what to do instead. By instilling good behavior, you help children conquer the undesirable behavior.

There are many reasons why parents may fail to teach a child. Work demands, too many children, and tension in the family are some of the hindrances to teaching that are most commonly reported by parents. But, as we stated earlier, parents cannot *not* teach. Parents need to take the effort to help a child learn correct behavior or risk having to deal with undesirable behavior. Even a few minutes of teaching each week can make a great difference in a child's behavior.

The second reason for a child not knowing what to do occurs when two parents say conflicting things. Children become confused and not sure what to do. Alternatively, children can be confused when parents act hypocritically telling the children to do one thing but doing the opposite themselves. The cure for this cause is obvious. Teach children and create a clear, consistent environment.

Conclusion

There are four causes of undesirable behavior: (1) developmental stages, (2) needs of the child, (3) something in the environment, and (4) the child's lack of knowledge. Of the four causes of behavior, only the first is determined by children, and they aren't aware of the development stage they are going through. The other three causes are beyond children's control. Children don't create their own needs, manipulate their environment, or know everything without being taught. If they didn't bring the causes about, you shouldn't be angry with them. Knowing the different causes of behavior and using the cues to identify them can help you to relax, to know how to best provide help, and to enjoy your children more.   ❀

Teaching Children about Sex and Reproduction

Attitudes and values are taught by how we choose to teach about certain subjects. For example, if a parent teaches sexual information in an embarrassed or nervous way, there is a good chance children will assimilate these same feelings about sex. Or, if parents believe sex is evil, base, and animalistic, these attitudes may also be communicated. This implies that the first step in teaching children needs to be a preparation of ourselves. We can learn to explicitly label the parts of the male and female anatomy and practice saying these and other terms until we feel comfortable doing so with our children. Someone suggested the idea to turn on the

shower and say these words aloud until no embar-
rassment is felt. You may laugh when you read this,
but it is a fairly good suggestion.

As you begin to formulate your method of
teaching, keep in mind what you want to accomplish.
You might , for example, decide that the objective is to
form a relationship with your children where you can
talk freely with each other. Subsequently, whenever
your children ask questions you can first reinforce the
behavior of coming to you and then try to tell them
what they want to know.

In addition to wanting them to have an accurate, factual knowledge about sex, another objective
might be to have your children learn from both parents, if both are available. There is much sons and
daughters can and should learn from both parents.
Both can be present in formal teaching times. Both will
be asked questions by the children. A third goal is to
teach according to a child's readiness to learn. Lastly,
in addition to believing that sex is a source of joy in
life, we suggest that most parents want their children
to have a deep understanding that their bodies are
sacred. The power of creating life is a sacred trust, and
expressing sexual love regularly and properly is necessary to form a lasting bond with a loved one.
Children need to learn to control sexual impulses now
as a means of preparing to make a relationship with a
marriage partner the best it can possibly be. There is
considerable evidence that the best sexual relationships are those where people live standards where

sexual behavior only occurs in a context of deep emotional commitment for the purposes of procreation and bonding two people together.

The following sections contain some information about development stages of children and some suggestions for what to teach during each stage. Also shown are some suggested ways to teach children.

First Concepts in Childhood: Ages 0-7

Development Stages

About birth to seven years of age children are curious and think about objects and their physical properties such as shape, texture, size and color. Children also organize ideas into concepts (i.e., what parts does a boy have or a girl). They want to know about sensations associated with objects.

Concepts

1. Teach about body parts using correct terms and differences between males and females.

2. Teach when to talk about parts of the body and when not to talk (i.e., at home with parents and not school class).

3. Teach concepts of modesty and how wonderfully our bodies are made.

4. Begin principles of conception, pregnancy, and prenatal growth.

Ways To Teach

1. Use baths or showers and children's questions as times to teach about the body.

2. Verbally explain times it is best to talk.

3. Use examples and positive comments about your own body and child's body to teach modesty and self-respect.

4. Use reading material about prenatal growth and childbirth. Use own pregnancy if appropriate.

5. Be loving, touch, and give affection.

Emotional Control and Pre-Puberty Physical Development: Ages 7-11

Development Stages

From ages seven to eleven children learn preliminary logical thinking, social skills, achieving a sense of relationship to other people, and learning to control emotions associated with personal life and social contacts.

Concepts

1. Teach about conception (sperm and egg unite) and reproduction.

2. Reinforce the need to talk openly with parents about questions children might have.

3. Use social events to teach modesty and appropriate conversation.

4. Help children learn to control their emotional impulses, avoid extreme or uncontrolled displays, be loving, learn to touch, and give affection.

Ways To Teach

1. Initiate conversation to learn about what a child knows. Reinforce your need to have a child talk to you.

2. Respond to questions as asked.

3. When a child exhibits extreme emotions, focus on the need to manage his or her impulses by sitting on a chair until calm, cooling off in a bedroom, and talking about his or her feelings.

Puberty and Early Adolescence: Ages 11-15

Development Stages

1. Increased interest in the body and in relating a person's body to such things as popularity, athletic skill, and attraction to opposite sex.

2. Increased awareness of physical changes and comparing themselves to others. They notice voice change, breast development, height, and hair on the body.

3. Increased self consciousness about "looks" and ability to relate how they look to other things such as other's respect and social values.

4. More importance is given to opinions of peers.

5. Children experience strong sexual desire for the first time.

6. Children can mentally see the logic behind reasons, they perceive cause and effect relationships.

Concepts

1. Teach about the changes that occur in puberty. (Menstruation, rapid growth that can be related to poor coordination, widening of shoulders

and narrowing of hips for boys, widening of hips for girls, enlargement of breasts for both boys and girls, development of body hair under arms and pubic area, and on boys' faces and arms)

2. Teach that "good looks" do not make a good person, and one must develop good values, standards of personal conduct, and modesty.

3. Teach social skills for making friends and talking with others so that popularity is achieved on some basis other than physical attraction.

4. Teach that individuals go through puberty at different rates: some early, some later, some rapidly, some slowly.

Ways To Teach

1. Obtain good information to use with your family. Elementary schools will have a good filmstrip.

2. Reinforce changes in children as positive by paying positive attention to their growth (e.g., "You sure have broad shoulders.")

3. Create teaching times where children are told about what to expect for boys and girls during puberty.

4. Share some of your experiences with puberty and its changes.

5. Initiate numerous conversations to ensure development of positive attitudes about a child's body, social success, and personal standards.

6. Frequently ask what ideas your children have about themselves.

7. Teach ways to manage sexual desire (i.e., avoid pornography, become involved in physical work).

Late Adolescence: Ages 15-18

Development Stages

1. Children can observe how they relate to others.

2. Reasons and ideas must appear logical to be accepted.

3. Perceived ability to make their choices is necessary for development of personal values. Attempts to force ideas will evoke resistance.

4. Social success increases in importance, especially attention from the opposite sex. Personal esteem is closely tied to feelings of being socially successful.

5. Children require abundant positive emotional support from parents.

6. Although children can understand correct principles, most have difficulty acting according to what they believe.

Concepts

1. Teach relationship of sex as a commitment to another person in marriage.

2. Too much sexual involvement too early cheapens and can ruin the companionship.

3. Physical attractiveness used to increase popularity will achieve temporary results.

4. How to hold expressions of intimacy within appropriate limits according to the state of responsible and legal commitment.

5. Sexual desire well-managed is a major part of preparing for success in marriage.

6. Techniques for avoiding compromising situations. One father gave a dime to his daughter with this instruction: "If a boy wants to go too far, give him the dime and ask him to call me. Tell him if I say it's OK then you can go ahead."

Ways To Teach

1. Share personal experience showing correct choices.

2. Ask children to tell you their decision about keeping chastity and virtue. Ask, "What have you decided to do?"

3. Emphasize positive examples of young people marrying properly.

4. Initiate long talks about affection, sex, and relationships with others.

5. Express confidence, support, and love.

6. Tell children clearly what you want for them and why without demanding or threatening.

7. Avoid critical comments about their looks, choices, or actions. Instead focus on desirable things you want them to do. ❀

Culture and Child Development

Usually, as children grow, their understanding expands from the parent-child relationship, to the immediate family, to an extended family, to their friends in the neighborhood, to their town or city, to their state, and to their country. As their participation in the activities of growing up increases, their understanding of their culture also increases. Family, media, church, schools, and friends transmit information about culture and how to participate in it. Child development is, therefore, influenced by culture. To understand child development, it is useful for us to be knowledgeable about how children develop in a cultural context.

The Cultural Context

Every culture has common ingredients. Each has a language and a system of communication, kinship relationships, customs and traditions, some form of government, formal laws which govern everyone, and informal rules which, though unspoken, exert considerable influence over how people act. In addition, the laws or rules in any culture are reinforced by disapproval and approval mechanisms. When children comply, they receive approval. When they do not, they receive disapproval. Examples of approval are affection and attention. Disapproval may include shunning, family punishment, and imprisonment.

A culture may have one or more religions which serve the purpose of giving direction to desirable behavior. The people in any culture may share some characteristics in common (e.g., language) but differ from one another in other respects. This is the diversity aspect of culture. To understand culture, therefore, we must appreciate how diverse and how similar are the peoples in the culture.

Participation in the Culture

In a context made up of these elements, children are born and reared. Their early family experiences are principally designed to teach them how to later participate in each aspect of their culture. They learn language, for example, and participate in kinship relationships. With their relatives, they learn how to participate in the customs of their culture. They discover approval and disapproval mechanisms and learn about conforming or non-conforming behaviors. They may also have experiences with fads and fashions which change from time to time.

The extent of a culture's influence on children depends upon how much or how well children participate in activities which are part of the cultural tradition. If a child cannot use language well, for example, he or she may not be able to benefit from the learning or training experiences of the culture in which the language is a part. Consider also, the idea that education is a means of transmitting cultural ideas. If a child does not participate meaningfully in educational activities, participation in the culture may be limited.

Cultural Notions about Child Development

Like any value, a culture will have some values or attitudes about child rearing and child care. These are taught in educational settings, demonstrated in methods of child care, and presented in the media. For example, Japanese parents are more likely to keep their children physically close to them than parents from the United States during the first three years of life. In the U.S., we value individuality and often treat our children in this manner. We also share some concept of what is "good" parenting or "bad" parenting. In any culture, when people demonstrate incompetent parenting, they receive disapproval from other cultural members. In similar ways, we may be approved of for parenting in the way each culture deems appropriate.

Beyond the foregoing, culture and child development are related in other ways. For example, the members of each culture informally establish certain times when development milestones should be demonstrated. Anyone watching a child develop will measure the developments by whether these milestones are manifest at about the times expected. In the United States, eighty percent agree that the best age for a man to marry is between twenty and twenty-five. The best time for a woman is between nineteen to twenty-four years of age. A "young" man is someone between the ages of eighteen and twenty-two and most think schooling should end between the ages of twenty and twenty-two.

Parents who are members of a culture will have awareness of these milestones and will often attempt to prepare their children to satisfy them. When children demonstrate the developmental milestones at the appropriate times, parents often feel more successful than when children do not.

Culture, Personality, and Values

All the participation in cultural events by parents and children inculcates values and ideals into each person about themselves and about the culture itself. As a result, we get a "national" personality, where members of a given culture are collectively stereotyped. Europeans may think, for example, that Americans are rich, vulgar, and loud. Americans may think that Latin

Americans are lazy, passionate, and not intelligent or industrious enough to rise above poverty. Europeans and Americans may think Asian people are shrewd, inscrutable, hard working, and pagan. Culture often dictates these negative stereotypes.

John Spielberg described some of these cultural values as they affect personality or social development. He compared three nationalities: American, Asian, and Latin American. He compared their values according to authority, orientation toward time, and orientation toward nature.

	United States	Latin America	Asia
authority	individualistic	autocratic	group
time	present-future	present	past-present
nature	subdue it	controlled by it	harmony with it

If we look at the table above, we can see that cultural values can be transmitted to individuals and can influence their social development. We can imagine there will be other influences a culture will have on individual socialization. Consider the power that comes from the following ideas: (1) everyone believes or does the same thing, (2) something must happen by a certain time because it is "expected," and (3) we think certain things in our culture are harmful to our family values. Forces resulting from ideas such as these are felt deeply by parents and affect how they participate in the social development of their children. ❀

Rules

Rules are formed when a person tries to understand how two or more things are related. Trying to understand the relationship introduces us to "ruleness." There are cognitive rules such as the way a child solves a problem or groups objects together. There are social rules for many situations and human relationships. There are also rules for games and play. Further, rules exist for the decisions a child makes as part of moral reasoning. In all of these cases, a rule is a statement of general principles which serves to guide behavior or to enable behavior to be understood.

Children's understanding of and response to rules appear to undergo a developmental sequence very similar to other aspects of child development. By understanding children's comprehension of rules and how they are affected by rules, we can increase our ability to help promote their development.

Rules, according to Gagne (1977), are a natural part of child development. They are a basic element of thought which every child learns. This learning appears to be related to the development of language and cognition. Further, children learn about rules from many sources and their response to rules can be influenced by friends, family, and the amount of exposure to social situations.

Because response to rules is a part of child development, there are no situations or styles of thought where rules are absent. There can only be differing rule forms or different responses to rules. Even if someone wishes to have no rules, a situation has been created with the special rule of not having any.

An example of the way the family environment can influence children's response to rules is shown in the study of the way deviance and schizophrenia are created. Children who exhibited behavioral rules deviant from their parents are often reared by parents who are very inconsistent and contradictory with rules. In this case, children form the rule that parental and societal rules do not apply to them.

Schizophrenia is a mental disorder where rules of thought the individual believes to be appropriate are not realistic. Such a person has rules, but they are altered from what most "normal" people use.

Researchers have found that parents can transmit these rules of thought to children. They communicate that a certain rule exists and children should follow it. After children follow the rule, they are criticized by a parent for following a rule the parent didn't create. The parents prevent the children from telling of the parental inconsistency. When these "double bind" conditions exist, children try to explain the situation to themselves by formulating an irrational rule of thought.

A negative family environment can adversely affect children, but a positive family environment can help children learn about varieties of rule forms and can promote a child's use of them. This is made more probable when parents understand the developmental sequence of children's response to rules.

Developmental Sequence

Stage I: Single Concept Learning (Ages 0-2)

Children do not know that rules exist. They learn single concepts and relate to each one by itself. Children are aware of very few ritual games, social conventions, or styles of thought. Consequently, a child is governed by demands while learning about people and situations.

Stage II: Rigid Adherence to Rules (Ages 4-7)

After developing the concept of rules, children recognize that rules apply to several situations. Children exhibit the rudiments of rule-governed problem solving and social exchange. Play becomes more formalized. Children consider rules, once established, to be sacred and untouchable. Changes in rules are made only if they appear to be new rules.

Stage III: Rule by Authority (Ages 7-11)

Children apply concepts of rules to the authority of adults. Respected adults are responded to as if whatever they say must be so. Rules, therefore, are more than the way games are played or the way people act in public. Rules are connected to authority and are used by those in authority to regulate others. Children's responses to rules are quite rigid. They accept few if any changes in explicit rules.

Stage IV: Flexibility and Cooperation (Ages 11 and older)

Adult authority is no longer accepted without question. Children begin to adjust rules to fit circumstances. They may rearrange the rules of a game to better accommodate some player. Satisfying human concerns can be more important than rigidly following the rules of a game. Children are able to create rules to suit their own unique purposes and include getting others involved to cooperate in making the rules. Diversity among children is more apparent and children can characterize one another by their willingness or unwillingness to cooperate in changing rules or creating new ones. ❖

A Dysfunctional Family

It is well-known that family experiences affect the development of children. It has only been in the last few years, however, that researchers have systematically studied the family to determine how it influences the development of children. In that process, we have learned some interesting things. One highly-significant idea is that the actual effects of a family on children are determined by factors within the child as well as within the family environment. For example, some children with excellent family environments do not do well as they grow up and struggle in many different ways. Further, some children in difficult family circumstances live and perform adequately or even very well. This tells us that to understand the role and influence of a family on children we must look at both family and children.

Family Dimensions

Most of us think about families as parents and children living together. We think about the differences between families with one parent, two parents, one child, many children, or all boys or all girls. These descriptions do not help us identify dysfunctional families. There are other ways to distinguish families that are dysfunctional from those that are effective. We can do this by evaluating family communication, work strategies, affection, rules, environmental sensitivity, and leadership and relationship styles.

Communication

All families are networks of communication. Families vary in how much information they communicate, whether they encourage everyone to participate, and what they communicate about. Families may also perpetuate communication problems when they interrupt each other, blame and criticize, speak sarcastically, or neglect communicating at all. Others may value communication highly so they avoid doing anything that will prevent positive communication from taking place.

Work

Families are places where work is required. Families may vary in how they divide the work, the standard of performance which is required, and how important work is compared with other family activities. For instance, some families work hard but also play hard. Others work more than they play and still others spend more time in leisure activity than at work.

Affectional System

The people in families develop and display regard and respect for one another. Some families may be openly demonstrative by touching, hugging, gazing at each other, and showing other forms of affection. Others may be less demonstrative and less open. The affectional system in families includes how families attend to the emotional behavior of family members. In some families feelings are expressed and understood, while in other families emotions tend to be ignored or unexpressed.

Rule System

Families have formal rules which are organized and discussed. They also have informal rules in the form of expected or routine practices. Some families will have many rules while others have only a few. In addition, families differ in terms of what they have rules about. One might have curfew rules and no rules about mealtimes while another would have rules about TV watching and none about getting work done. Most families have a discipline system where parents or caretakers express approval or disapproval for what children do and how they act. Families can be understood in terms of how they establish a rule system and enforce it.

Environmental Sensitivity

Some families will explore the world and bring home interesting things to discuss and share. Others are less aware of their environment and might be frightened of it. Therefore, they are less likely to venture out and learn. In addition, families can be understood in terms of the types of activities they participate in. Some may actively participate in religious activities while others participate in non-religious social activities.

Leadership and Relationship Styles

People in families form relationship styles. These relationships are demonstrated in the way leadership is exerted in the family. Leadership may be democratic, where most family members have a say in the way the family is governed, or authoritarian, where one parent or both make demands on children. In any event, all families will have a leadership and relationship style which characterizes the family.

How Dysfunctional Families Differ from Effective Families

Having learned about some family dimensions, we can proceed to our understanding of the characteristics of a dysfunctional family. The term "dysfunctional" means the family is not able to promote the positive development of its members. Instead, family members are involved in practices that hurt their growth. Researchers have given names to certain conditions which prevent positive development from taking place. Notice that these conditions exist because the family members do not have a broad or clear understanding of children and the knowledge of how to promote development.

Enmeshment

This dysfunctional condition exists when children believe their thoughts must be the same as other family members. Enmeshment is created in several ways. Excessive fear of disapproval is a leading cause. In addition, when families fail to recognize individual traits, needs, desires, and emotions of family members, then it is possible for one person to think he or she is simply like everyone else. In healthy families, there is strong emphasis on both togetherness and individuality. Individuals are asked to make choices where they are primarily responsible. In addition, communication in the family allows for individual opinions.

Abuse

Abuse can be anything which removes a person's sense of self-control and self-confidence. In dysfunctional families, there may be one or more types of abuse. This may be physical, where an older, bigger person physically hurts a younger, weaker person.

Abuse may be emotional, where words are demeaning and hurtful or where affection and attention is withdrawn or used to exploit someone. Abuse may also be sexual, where one person is used and exploited for the gratification of another without having a chance to make choices or be aware of the consequences of those events. In many instances extreme levels of stress from outside pressures are related to the incidence of abuse. In healthy families, relationships are established for the welfare of individuals. Therefore, how they act toward each other is moderate and non-exploitative. Methods of discipline are democratic and there are open displays of affection which are not withdrawn as a result of misbehavior.

Excessive Dependency

Children begin life dependent on adults. This dependency is recognized and accepted because children are not able to care for themselves. As they mature, however, children typically want to do things for themselves and make demands to do so. The parent-child attachment is sufficiently intense that unless parents and children are sensitive to the development of independence, children can learn excessive dependency. This is manifest by helplessness, inability to leave the home, passivity when in proximity to parents, failure to achieve, irresponsibility, deviance from family rules which appears to require parents to exert control, confusion and indecision, and separation distress when leaving parents.

These conditions can be caused when parents do not encourage gradual separation between themselves and their children. Further, some parents assume excessive responsibility for their children and attempt to prevent failures by rescuing them from hurtful situations rather than letting children solve their own problems. Parents may also indulge their children without setting behavior limits and enforcing them. When children are indulged and have no standards to live up to, they acquire the belief that they need only be nice and pleasant to be adequate.

Dependency can be enduring. There is some evidence that dependent children become dependent adults. This means they will seek relationships with others which approximate the emotional conditions of their early family experience. They may, for example, seek a marital partner whom they can be dependent upon, and they will be uncomfortable when they are asked to act decisively and independently.

Mental and Emotional Illness

For many years, researchers did not make any connection between dysfunctional families and emotional and mental problems. Now, however, there is a clear link between such family problems as chemical abuse. Forty percent of chemically abusing teens have parents who abuse chemicals such as alcohol and drugs. Some forms of depression appear to be inherited, but other depression is learned from parents' examples. When families have communication which is not logical or based on reality, children can learn a form of irrationality which manifests itself in schizophrenic thought disorders. The family appears to believe something and children assume that it is factual. An example is the famous case of the Emmanuel David family, where the father kept his children isolated from any source of information, proclaimed himself to be a prophet or the Holy Ghost, and then jumped from a hotel window followed by four of his children and his wife. Two children survived.

In contrast, healthy families have a fairly open communication system with the world around them. They may screen out information which does not promote their specific values, but they are usually aware of and communicate with people and institutions outside the family.

Incompetence

Some parents do not have basic child care or organizational skills. Therefore, they are not able to organize a family or care for children in ways which promote development. In these cases, families do not have routines of care such as bedtimes or mealtimes. They do not have methods which allow them to identify and respond to children's needs in terms of clothing, feeding, emotional support, and so on. Children's physical and mental growth may be retarded. In addition, they may have very limited ability to function in social situations or achieve educationally or at work.

Healthy families, of course, have effective child care methods and organize their families in ways which are conducive to healthy development. They have positive care routines, set predictable activities for the family, and nurture child growth. ❋

The Endocrine Glands

All the physiological functions of humans are coordinated and regulated by the nervous system. To this system there must be added a special integrating mechanism of chemical regulation. These chemical regulators are called hormones and are produced by endocrine glands. The endocrine glands play an especially important part in coordinating and regulating the physiological processes of the whole person.

The endocrine glands do not constitute an organ system, but are referred to as the transmission to the various tissues. Hormones exert profound effects on certain tissues and are needed in relatively small amounts to produce their effect. The tissue on which a specific hormone exerts its effect is called the target tissue. A state of balance and a reciprocal interaction normally exist between the various glands. One gland may simultaneously stimulate many glands, which may produce a series of stimulations and inhibitions. Thus, where one endocrine gland can stimulate another, the gland that is stimulated may have an inhibiting effect on the stimulator.

As in the relationship between estrogen and the follicle-stimulating hormone, when one decreases the other increases, and vice versa. It is important to have a basic understanding of how hormones work because they play an important role in a person's physical growth and development, metabolism, reproductive cycle, sexuality, emotional life, and personality. We will briefly study the following endocrine glands: (1) pituitary, (2) thyroid, (3) parathyroids, (4) adrenals, (5) pancreas, and (6) gonads.

The Pituitary

The pituitary is located in the brain. Generally the gland is divided into the anterior, intermediate, and posterior lobes. The anterior pituitary secretes hormones that mainly influence other endocrine glands and best illustrates the reciprocal relationship that exists within this system. These hormones are referred to as tropins and are carried by the blood to other target glands where they aid in the maintenance of the glands and stimulate them to produce their own hormones. Six hormones are secreted by this part of the pituitary: the growth hormone, the lactogenic hormone, the follicle-stimulating hormone, the luteinizing hormone, the thyrotrophic hormone, and the adrenocorticotrophic hormone.

The growth hormone, also known as somatotrophin (STH) functions to stimulate the growth of the long bones and muscles. Excess production of growth hormone during childhood or adolescence results in giantism. Normally, the growth hormone is active only up to the time of maturity. Growth hormone in excess suppresses gonadotrophic hormones. If the testes and adrenals in the male or adrenal glands in the female do not develop normally in puberty, epiphyseal closure of the long bones, which is dependent on the male hormone, fails to take place, and a person can continue to grow to seven or eight feet.

Should the hyperfunction occur after epiphyseal closure, there is no further increase in linear growth but an increase in the width of bone. This results in an unusual thickening of the hands and feet, prominence of the jaw, and enlargement of the nose, and is called acromegaly.

The lactogenic hormone (LTH), also known as prolactin, stimulates growth of the mammary glands and the follicle-stimulating hormone (FSH) stimulates the graafian follicle in the ovaries to mature and produce estrogen and stimulate sperm formation in the male. The luteinizing hormone (LH) causes ovulation and development of the corpus luteum and production of progesterone in the female and stimulates testosterone production by the testes in the male. These hormones are essential at the time of puberty and throughout the reproductive life of the ovaries for continued graafian follicle development and ovulation. FSH is carried to the ovaries by way of the blood stream where it stimulates the ovarian follicle to mature and estrogen secretion is stimulated.

As a result of estrogen secretion, changes occur in the secondary sexual characteristics. At the time of ovulation, which is initiated by the combined action of FSH and LH, the level of estrogen reaches its peak and suppresses the secretion of FSH. As the concentration of FSH in the bloodstream falls, its stimulating effect on the graafian follicle is decreased and the secretion of estrogen is decreased. As the concentration of estrogen falls, more FSH is secreted, resulting in the development of another follicle and more estrogen secretion.

LTH seems to be responsible for causing the corpus luteum to produce progesterone. Since progesterone is necessary for the growth and maintenance of the endometrium in the uterus, it is necessary for the corpus luteum to be sustained until the embryo has been able to establish itself in the uterus and has begun to develop. If the corpus luteum is not maintained for any reason, the endometrium sloughs off as the menstrual flow. If the woman is pregnant, the implanted fertilized ovum is carried away with the debris.

A reciprocal relationship exists between the levels of LH and LTH and progesterone similar to that

206 ✤ Understand Child Development

which exists between FSH and estrogen. As the level of progesterone increases in the blood, the secretion of LH and LTH is suppressed. As a result, the corpus luteum begins to fade and the concentration of progesterone decreases. If the egg is not fertilized, the supplemental supply of progesterone produced at the site of implantation in the uterus will not be forthcoming from the placental membranes, and the corpus luteum disintegrates and the endometrium sloughs off. The waning in the concentration of the progesterone stimulates the pituitary to secrete more LH and LTH.

The thyrotrophic hormone functions to maintain the thyroid gland and stimulates it to produce the hormone thyroxine. Too much of this hormone causes excessive production of the thyroid hormone, and thus produces all the symptoms of excessive thyroid activity (hyperthyroidism). On the other hand, a deficiency of thyrotrophic hormone causes the thyroid to atrophy.

The adrenocorticotrophic hormone (ACTH) stimulates the secretion of cortical hormones by the adrenal cortex. Excess production of ACTH stimulates the adrenal cortex to produce steroids, which causes water retention in the face and gives a characteristic roundness of the face sometimes described as "pig eye" or "moonface." There is also usually an increased growth of hair on the face.

The intermediate lobe secretes a hormone known as the melanocyte-stimulating hormone, or MSH. It acts in the dispersion of pigment granules in the melanocytes, which are important in the darkening of the skin, as in tanning.

The posterior lobe secretes two active substances: vasopressin and oxytocin. Vasopressin acts to elevate blood pressure by constricting the peripheral blood vessels and also promotes resorption of water by the kidneys. It has been used in cases of surgical shock in conjunction with other drugs to elevate the blood pressure. Oxytocin stimulates smooth muscle contraction, particularly of the uterus. It is therefore used in obstetrics to prevent postpartum hemorrhage resulting from an overly relaxed uterus.

The Thyroid

In contrast to the pituitary gland, the thyroid gland has only two hormones: thyroxine and triiodothyronine. The primary action of thyroid hormones is on regulating the metabolic rate. These hormones directly increase the rate of oxidation of foodstuffs within the cells of the tissues. Many normal functions of the organism are dependent on thyroid secretion. These include water and mineral metabolism and the normal function of the nervous system, muscular systems, and circulatory system. All these functions are disturbed with either a deficiency or excess of the hormone.

Abnormalities associated with the thyroid gland are due to a deficiency of iodine, the essential element of the thyroid hormone, to an insufficient production of the hormone itself, or to an over-activity of the gland with the liberation of an excessive amount. A deficiency of iodine in the diet is frequently accompanied by an enlargement of the gland which is called a goiter. In this condition the thyroid is enlarged, apparently to compensate for the lack of iodine.

A deficiency of thyroid hormone, referred to as hypothyroidism, produces a number of symptoms depending on the degree of deficiency and the age at which it occurs. Lack of thyroid hormone in very early childhood leads to cretinism, a condition characterized by cessation of mental and physical development, slow heart rate, poor appetite, and constipation.

Thyroid insufficiency occurring later in childhood results in juvenile myxedema. Characteristically, the child shows a tendency to be stout, short, and squatty. The head is proportionately larger than normal for the age of the child and is attached to the trunk by a short neck. In an adult, hypothyroidism gives rise to the condition known as myxedema. In true myxedema, the face is quite expressionless, puffy, and pallid. Both the mental and physical processes slow down.

Excessive thyroid function, known as hyperthyroidism, results from enlargement of the gland, with over-production and excessive release of thyroid hormone. The most characteristic symptoms, in addition to goiter, are nervousness, irritability, purposeless movements, fatigue, loss of weight, increased heart rate, elevated metabolic rate, and emotional instability.

The Parathyroids

The parathyroids produce a hormone that plays a vital role in the metabolism of calcium and phosphorus. The symptoms of hypothyroidism are muscle weakness, tetany, and irritability.

The Adrenals

The adrenals are two pyramid-shaped structures lying one on each side of the body, close to the upper part of the kidney. Each gland consists of two functionally distinct parts: a central portion called the medulla, and a surrounding zone of tissue called the cortex. The only function of the adrenal medulla is the secretion of epinephrine. In general, epinephrine has the same effect on a person as stimulation of the sympathetic nerves. The secretion of the adrenal medulla is under control of the sympathetic nervous system and in emergency situations or exposure to stress, such as injury, excessive muscular exercise, infection, hemorrhage, cold, fever, burn, and nervous shock, epinephrine is discharged into the blood. The increase of epinephrine helps the organism to re-establish the physiological balance that has been disturbed. Prolonged stimulation can cause exhaustion of the epinephrine stores.

The adrenal cortex produces hormones which are necessary for life. The adrenal cortex produces many hormones, but only three are of interest to us: cortisone, androgen, and estrogen. Cortisone helps maintain water balance in the tissues and helps the body resist infection and cope with the effects of long-term stress. It is often a treatment for rheumatoid arthritis, rheumatic fever, and leukemia. The side effect of this hormone used therapeutically is that the body retains a lot of water and the patient looks quite puffy.

The adrenal cortex secretes both male and female hormones. Certain tumors of the adrenals cause the production of increased amounts of these hormones, giving rise to physical abnormalities referred to as the adrenogenital syndrome. In the young male with adrenogenital syndrome, there is precocious development of the penis and pubic hair, along with advanced bone age and early and increased growth rate. A girl born with adrenogenital syndrome may show an enlarged clitoris and may be mistaken for a male; thus she may be raised as a boy. In the adult female with adrenogenital syndrome, there is repression of female characteristics with a prominence of male characteristics.

The Pancreas

The pancreas produces the hormone insulin. Insulin promotes the removal of glucose from the blood and makes it available to be converted to glycogen in the muscles and liver. An excessive amount of insulin in the blood commonly results from improper insulin medication and occasionally from tumors. The resulting symptoms are caused by the fall in blood sugar, a condition referred to as hypoglycemia.

Drowsiness and yawning usually occur, and the hypo-glycemic person may become excited, perspire, or appear to be under the influence of alcohol. Convulsive seizures may occur, and finally the patient may go into a coma and die. If adequate amounts of glucose are given to the person, the symptoms go away. The administration of insulin to diabetic patients rapidly restores the ability to oxidize carbo-hydrates and to form glycogen.

When there is a deficiency of insulin, the utiliza-tion of glucose decreases but the level of blood glucose rapidly rises. This produces a condition known as hyperglycemia which results in a series of symptoms referred to as diabetes mellitus. Diabetes is a metabolic disease characterized by a disturbance in the metabo-lism of carbohydrates, protein, and fat. The disease usu-ally leads to weight loss, kidney failure, and blindness.

Gonads

Ovaries

In females, two ovaries are situated deep in the pelvic cavity, one each side of the uterus. Each ovary represents the female gonad in which the ova are pro-duced. Within the ovaries are a number of ovarian fol-licles. It has been estimated that there are approxi-mately four hundred thousand immature follicles in both ovaries at birth. Beginning at puberty, the folli-cles mature, one approximately every twenty-eight to thirty days.

Deviations from the normal course of menstruation are not uncommon. Menorrhagia is a condition characterized by an abnormal loss of blood during the monthly period. It is usually caused by endocrine or ovarian functional disturbances. Metrorrhagias are irregular hemorrhages. The hemorrhage may appear before the menstrual period, in the middle of the interval, or after the menstrual period. Amenorrhea is the term used to denote the absence of menstruation. The most common cause of amenorrhea is pregnancy, but other causes can be excessive physical exercise or anorexia. Menopause is that period in the female reproductive cycle when menstrual flow ceases. It can occur at any time after menarche, but on the average the onset is around forty-seven to forty-eight years.

If the ovaries of the normal female are removed before puberty because of some disease or have been rendered inactive by x-ray therapy, the child never develops the secondary sexual characteristics, and the sexual organs remain immature. Growth continues at a normal rate but does not show the usual spurt associated with puberty. The individual ends up with skeletal configuration typical of eunuchs; the length of the lower limbs is much greater than that of the trunk. Removal of the ovaries after puberty will also cause changes; the breasts usually atrophy, growth of hair on the face and body may occur, the body configuration of the female becomes more masculine, and sexual drive may decrease. The administration of estrogen is highly satisfactory in the treatment of eunuchoidism, as it will cause development of the secondary sexual characteristics.

The Testes

In males, the testicles are two small, flattened, oval-shaped glands which are situated in the scrotum. The testicles are composed of a number of lobules. Each lobule is composed of several seminiferous tubules. There are eight hundred or more tubules in the testicles. The testes, like the ovaries, have a dual function of producing sperm and sex hormone.

Hypogonadism is the condition of total loss of hormone activity of the testes. It occurs in castrated men and with insufficient activity of the testes due to a deficiency of the pituitary. Castration before puberty or hypogonadism is usually followed by an excessive longitudinal growth of bones. Sex hormones stimulate the fusion of the epiphyses; thus, in their absence there is a delayed fusion, producing disproportionate growth of long bones. Hypogonadism in the male usually causes an accumulation of fat in the mammary region, around the hips, and below the waist. Early hypogonadism leads to a retardation of development of the penis, prostate, seminal vesicles, and vas deferens.

Hypergonadism refers to overactivity of the gonads, which leads to excessive development of the genitalia, secondary sexual characteristics, and the body as a whole. Such men would have unusually broad shoulders, narrow hips, extremely muscular

214 ❀ Understand Child Development

bodies, inordinately large sexual organs, and excessive body hair.

Conclusion

Many times children do not act exactly the way their parents think they should. They appear slow in their movements, look lazy, or seem to not be paying attention to what is going on. Many times this is caused by hormones inside of the child. When a parent assigns blame to the child as though he or she could control these behaviors, it makes the child's life miserable and he or she cannot do anything about that.

There is a sort of wisdom of the body that children discover very early. They adapt their lifestyles and activities to what their bodies will allow them to do. Take for instance the case of a child who has low levels of thyroxin. He will be slow and lethargic, and any excess amount of activity, as in running races or something of that nature, totally depletes his energy source.

As this child grows up and starts to play with children on the block and engages in strong physical activities, his body pays a terrific price for that, so he learns to avoid those kind of things and picks out activities such as reading or working at a desk where he doesn't have as much pain. The first thing that parents need to do when a child has some kind of problem caused by a hormonal imbalance is to see if there is some way that it can be corrected. If there isn't, they should be very patient and supportive of the child.

One of the developmental phenomena that are regulated by hormones is the age that somebody sexually matures, or goes through puberty. It would be nice if everyone's body matured at the same age, on the thirteenth birthday, for instance. But that isn't how it works. People that deviate from the norm of physical maturation carry a lot of stress. For instance, an early developing girl who matures in fourth or fifth grade or a late developing boy need a lot of support.

While growing up, one boy was very late in developing. It wasn't any fault of his, of course. He happened to get some genes from his parents that dictated this to his body. When he was seventeen his father, who was also a late-developing boy, tried to give him some encouragement by saying, "Don't worry that you're smaller than your friends. I grew six inches when I was twenty-two." Unfortunately, this boy heard the last part of the sentence and not the first part, and nearly jumped off the roof of his house. He told his dad, "If I have to wait 'til I'm twenty-two to finally grow up and look like other guys, I'm just going to kill myself."

The principle to remember is that parents need to be informative and supportive. It is not very helpful to overreact by racing around trying to find doctors who will correct abnormalities in the hormone system that are within the normal range of deviation. ❀

GLAND	HORMONES	FUNCTIONS	DEFICIENCY	EXCESS
Anterior Pituitary	Growth Hormone or Somatotrophin	Controls growth of bone & muscle; anabolic effect on nitrogen metabolism; carbohydrate and fat metabolism; elevates glycogen stores of skeletal & cardiac muscle	Dwarfism	Giantism acromegaly
	Thyrotrophic Hormone	Controls the rate of iodine uptake by thyroid tissue and influences the synthesis of thyroxine from diiodotyrosine	Atrophy of thyroid	Enlargement of thyroid
	Adrenocorticotrophic Hormone	Stimulates the secretion of cortical hormones by the adrenal cortex	Atrophy of adrenal cortex	Unknown
	Prolactin or Lactogenic Hormone	Controls proliferation of the mammary gland and initiation of milk secretion; prolongs the functional life of the corpus luteum, the secretion of progesterone	Infertility	Persistent lactation

GLAND	HORMONES	FUNCTIONS	DEFICIENCY	EXCESS
	Gonadotrophin	**Ovary:** Controls formation of corpus luteum, secretion of progesterone; probably acts in conjunction with FSH. **Testes:** Stimulates the interstitial cell of Leydig, promoting the production of androgen	Infertility	Abnormal sexual development
	Follicle-Stimulating Hormone	**Ovary:** Controls growth of ovarian follicles; functions with LH to cause estrogen secretion and ovulation. **Testes:** Has possible action on seminiferous tubules to promote spermatogenesis	Infertility	Premature sexual development
Posterior Pituitary	Antidiuretic	Affects water content of tissues; increases blood pressure	Excessive urine formation	Unknown
	Oxytocin	Stimulates uterine contraction; stimulates milk-producing cells of the mammary glands	Slow labor	Unknown

GLAND	HORMONES	FUNCTIONS	DEFICIENCY	EXCESS
Thyroid	Thyroxin	Regulates general metabolism	Cretinism in children; lowered metabolic rate; weakness	Exophtalimic goiter; increased metabolic rate; weakness
Pancreas	Insulin	Carbohydrate metabolism	Diabetes mellitus; insulin shock; diabetic coma	Hunger & weakness; uses up sugar
Adrenal Cortex	Cortisone	Maintains: a. water balance in tissues b. carbohydrate balance c. resistance to stress	Addison's Disease	Masculinizes boys and women
	Androgen	Assists in sexual development	Retardation or lack of sexual development	Masculinity in females; unknown in males
	Estrogen	Assists in sexual development	Retardation or lack of sexual development	Femininity in males; upsets menstrual cycle in females

GLAND	HORMONES	FUNCTIONS	DEFICIENCY	EXCESS
Gonads				
Ovaries	Estrogen	Female secondary sexual characteristics; stimulates reproductive organs to develop	Retardation of sexual development	Unknown
	Progesterone	Development of uterus in preparation for pregnancy	Miscarriage of early embryo	Unknown
Testes	Testosterone (Androgen)	Male secondary sexual characteristics; stimulates reproductive organs to develop	Retardation of sexual development	Unknown
Placenta	Placental Gonadotrophin (embryonic portions)	Suppresses production of gonadotrophin, thereby preventing further ovulation	Unknown	Unknown
	Estrogen	Seems to counteract effect of LTH upon mammary glands, preventing milk formation	Unknown	Unknown
	Progesterone	Takes over function of corpus luteum progesterone as it is diminished	Miscarriage of fetus	Unknown

Families as Socializers

When a child is born, he or she is born not only into a family but into a society. Each society has different rules and expectations for how it thinks its members should act. A child does not know these expectations when he or she is born and has to be taught while growing up. Anciently, the only socializing influence on a child was the family, usually the extended family. A child had parents, aunts, uncles, cousins, and grandparents all living in close proximity. They taught the child the rules of the family and how to work and cooperate. There were no schools or government policies or mass media presentations. The bulk of a child's time was spent with family members who socialized him or her. As the family became more nuclear and moved away from close contact with siblings and parents, other socializing agents came into existence.

Consider the following major socializing agents:
- family
- friends
- church
- school
- TV
- magazines
- government policies
- cultural heritage

We want you to evaluate each of these socializers as to how much control a parent can have over them. Do you think a parent has no control, some control, or total control over each of them?

The reason you are doing this is because today's parents know their children are going to be exposed to messages and lifestyles different from what they teach in the home and they panic. But if parents can control some of the other messages their children hear they won't have to be as nervous. Parenting can be grim when you feel you have no control over the impact other people or institutions have on your children.

Now that you've made your judgments, let us tell you what can happen. You can have near total control over the family. A husband and wife should be able to send a unified message to their children regarding values and other significant aspects of life. It's possible to have total control over church, not by altering a church, but by finding a church that teaches the same things you do.

Similarly, you can have great control over the school, not by telling teachers what to teach, but by finding a school that teaches and reinforces the things that you do. To find such a school might mean your children would go to a private school. The ultimate private school, one that you would definitely have total control over, would be a home school. There are thousands of families who teach their children at home, especially through the elementary school years. In a home school, parents have total control because they decide the curriculum, choose the texts, and so on. The option of home schooling your children helps parents gain control over what their children are exposed to, but this option isn't for every family.

Unless you are really into censoring things, you won't have much control over what your children are exposed to in the media, and you cannot completely control who their friends are. You will have very little control over government policies. You don't have to be in control of all these socializers to have a happy life. If you can control just a few, then you are going to be able to raise great children wherever you live.

The impact of the family can be more important and powerful than any other socializer, especially in the long term. There may be short periods of time when friends will have more influence, but if you've bonded with your children and have a loving and nurturing home, then your family will be the most powerful socializer. And remember, your family is the first social institution your child encounters. He who teaches first, teaches best.

Researchers have looked at many parental qualities to see which ones seem to make a difference in terms of how children develop. Many believe there are three qualities that account for most of the differences. The first is the amount of control parents exert over their children. It can vary from very little control (autonomy) to total control. The second quality is the amount of warmth parents show to children. It varies from aloof to hostile to loving. The third quality is the amount of anxiety parents feel regarding their role as parents. It varies from high anxiety (neurotic) to low anxiety (calm).

There are many reasons why parents might have low control over their children: fear (they avoid making choices), anger (their children aren't worth their time), and trust (they believe their children are able to make wise choices on their own). There are also several reasons why a person may feel high or low anxiety or high or low warmth. Because there are several good reasons for each state of mind, this model isn't perfect, but it can teach us some general truths. We have tried to visualize for you how these three dimensions interact. Look at Figure 2 on pages 226-228. Picture that all parents can be represented by a round ball. We can divide the ball into a left part and a right part and let those parts represent hostile and warm parents, respectively. Finally, we can divide the ball into a front part and a back part and let those parts represent high-anxiety and low-anxiety parents, respectively. The two circles in the figure represent the front and back parts (we can't draw in these dimensions). This creates eight different parental styles. We have labeled each one of them.

A parent who is hostile, has low control, and is highly anxious is a rejecting parent. A parent who has low control but is warm, nurturant, and calm is a democratic parent. Parents don't divide equally into each of these eight types, but there are families of each type. Each of these types describes family climates and different kinds of children that come from them. Pages 228-230 list some of the characteristics of each family type and the children they produce.

In only two of these eight family climates do children thrive and become the very best they can be. Children can usually learn to cope with any kind of a parental setting, even a rejecting or dictatorial family, as long as that family is consistent in its behavior. Children can learn to deal with abusive parents. They usually don't wither up and die psychologically, but they don't reach their potential. The two types of family climates where children thrive are democratic and authoritative. Notice what is similar in those two family types. Both of these family types have parents who are calm, relaxed, confident, warm, nurturant, and expressive.

It is in these two types of families where true bonding takes place. Bonding is an interesting phenomenon. When children bond to their parents they identify with them, they want to be like them, and they adopt their value systems. If you create a family that is loving and expressive, you are relaxed and enjoy being a parent. The odds are that you will have good children who will bond to you. This doesn't mean that parenting is going to be easy, but you will enjoy the hard work of being a parent and will enjoy your children. And you will have minimal worries about raising your children, no matter what other socializing voices your children may hear.

One belief that raises future parents' anxiety is that they can't be successful if they have a non-traditional family. The traditional family, which is diminishing year by year, consists of a father who works, a mother in the home, and a small number of children. Non-traditional families include single-parent families and families with working mothers. Some people think that because they do not have a traditional family they are not good people.

Good children are being raised in all types of families. There appear to be few differences in the children that come from families where mothers work and families where the mother is in the home. Good children come from both kinds of families and disturbed children come from both kinds of families. The important thing for a mother who decides to work is her attitude toward working. If a mother is happy with her work, then her attitude shows through in her parenting, and she will be relaxed and enjoy her children. Working outside of the home does not mean a mother has abandoned her children. Children actually benefit from good pre-school experience where they interact with peers as opposed to interacting only with parents and brothers and sisters. They can learn things with peers, even at the age of two and three, that they cannot learn at home. There aren't any general differences in children whose mothers work and are happy than in children whose mothers don't work and are happy, except that the former children tend to be a little more independent.

FIGURE 2
PARENT-CHILD INTERACTION MODEL
Wesley Becker (1964)

Three variables are used in the Parent-Child Interaction Model: support, control, and anxiety. By using these three variables, the following outcomes are possible.

LC = Low Control, HC = High Control,
LA = Low Anxiety, HA = High Anxiety,
LS = Low Support, HS = High Support

LC, LS, LA = Permissive
LC, LS, HA = Rejecting
HC, LS, LA = Rigid Controlling
HC, LS, HA = Dictatorial

LC, HS, LA = Democratic
LC, HS, HA = Overindulgent
HC, HS, LA = Authoritative
HC, HS, HA = Overprotective

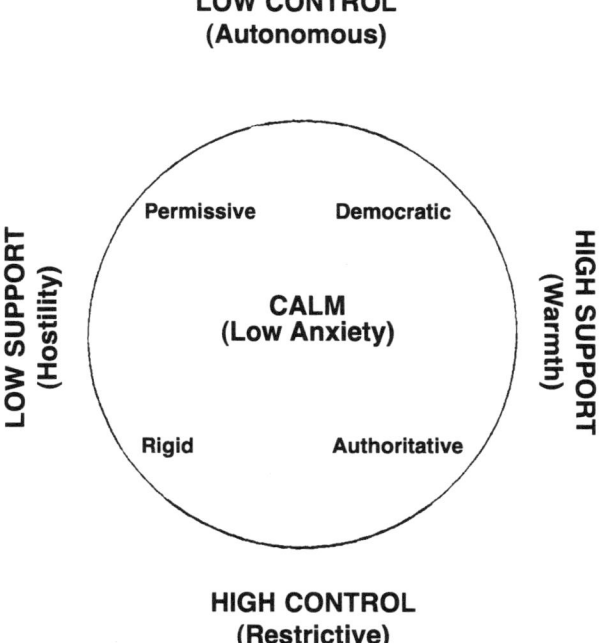

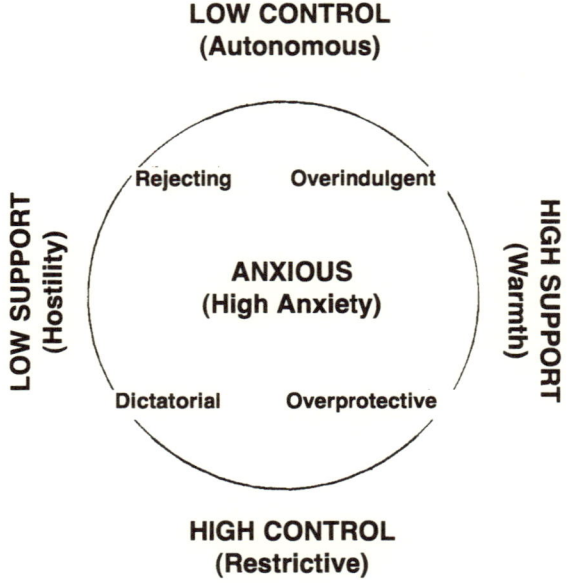

LOW CONTROL
(Autonomous)

LOW SUPPORT
(Hostility)

Rejecting   Overindulgent

ANXIOUS
(High Anxiety)

HIGH SUPPORT
(Warmth)

Dictatorial   Overprotective

HIGH CONTROL
(Restrictive)

Characteristics of Parents and Children

Permissive (LC, LS, LA)

Parents: Self-centered, selfish, show lack of concern and lack of warmth, often highly inconsistent in their use of discipline.

Children: Many delinquents come from this type of home and generally display aggressive or uncontrolled behavior.

Rigid Controlling (HC, LS, LA)

Parents: Restrictive and hostile, but do not allow the children to show hostility toward them.

Children: Shy, socially withdrawn, anxious, neurotic, and self-punishing.

Democratic (LC, HS, LA)

Parents : Warm and supportive, limits and rules set by parents AND children. The concept of a family council is often used. Show confidence in children and cooperate with them.

Children: Creative and independent, socially outgoing, achievements are self-rewarding, moderately compliant, non-conformist. Also considered by some as rowdy, not submissive, lacking obedience.

Authoritative (HC, HS, LA)

Parents: A few highly-structured rules and limits established for the children's benefit, very methodical in decision-making, high standards of excellence established within reasonable limits, push children to function at peak of their abilities, and generally warm, confident, supportive, and success oriented.

Children: Usually "model" children. They have a strong conscience, very compliant, and respect persons with authority.

Rejecting (LC, LS, HA)

Parents: Feel the world is out to get them and see their children as the main source of their anxiety—children are a symbol of the parents' inability to cope with the real world.

Children: Reflect parents' anxiety, motivated to perform antisocial behavior, socially punitive, and aggressive.

Dictatorial (HC, LS, HA)

Parents: Highly restrictive, punitive, and similar to Rigid Controlling parents. They try to appease their anxiety by striking out at their children. The anxiety and frustration is caused by sources outside the family.

Children: Like those of Rigid Controlling children.

Overindulgent (LC, HS, HA)

Parents: They fear that they will frustrate their children so they set no limitations or restrictions on them. Submit to all of children's desires.

Children: Extremely independent, manipulators, antisocially aggressive, little development of conscience which causes a lack of compliance and mischievousness.

Overprotective (HC, HS, HA)

Parents: Lives centered completely around children, do not use physical punishment, use love withdrawal and emotional manipulation to control children, establish high standards of achievement, remove obstacles that might cause misbehavior.

Children: Set unrealistic goals for themselves in an attempt to please parents, highly compliant and dependent on parents, strong conscience development in order to protect against parents' withdrawal of love. ❀

Self-Regulation

Self-regulation allows an individual to achieve a desired result by exerting inner control when there are distractions, persuaders, or other influences that must be resisted in order to do so. It has also been called impulse control, deferred gratification, self-control, and resistance to temptation.

Self-regulation itself is an adoptive strategy which people develop to control the amount of environmental pressure they feel. Humans make plans to act intentionally and appear to devise strategies that will help them carry out their plans while they are in the association of others, while they are confronted with other attractive alternatives, and while motivational levels fluctuate.

There is some indication that this develops spontaneously. A child's awareness of self-regulation strategies appears after eight years of age. For example, Mischel (1978) reported a study designed to identify how pre-schoolers, third graders, and sixth graders postponed pleasure. After age eight, children were significantly better able to identify their strategies than were the pre-school children.

The development of self-regulation has been associated with the formation of inner speech. This internal dialogue appears to be a necessary part of forming strategies of self-control. The most detailed theory of self-regulation is described by Lev Vygotsky (1962). He proposed that, at first, a child is regulated by adults and learns adult language and style of thought. During the time this is taking place, a child is highly influenced by the context in which he or she performs. This means, for example, a child would pay more attention to a mother's instructions than to cues helping to solve a problem. As inner speech develops, a child's attention shifts from environmental cues to those inherent in solving a problem. The child, therefore, becomes more self-regulated.

Vygotsky suggested that this development takes place in four steps. The first involves adult-child interactions, when the child fails to correctly interpret the adult's speech, resulting in failure to adequately regulate performance. This evolves into a situation where the child more adequately comprehends adult speech and successfully performs because of the regulation of the parent. The adult-child interaction, however, teaches the child to recognize the cues necessary to perform a task. The third level consists of the child making a transition from parental- to self-regulation. The child senses the cues necessary to perform the task and performs them with some minimal interaction with the adult for reassurance. Level four is simply a further advancement to the point that a child performs the task, using inner thought to succeed at the task.

Based on Vygotsky's theory, it appears possible to enhance this development by rehearsal and by effective adult involvement. Children can be helped to focus on the requirements of a task, encouraged to perform them, and directed to evaluate their inner speech related to the task. Such activities help focus thoughts on what a child intends to do, thus minimizing the effects of distractions.

Sequence of Development

Initial Comprehension (Ages 0-3)

A child has minimal understanding of his or her thoughts and also fails to accurately understand language meanings of other regulators.

Interaction (Ages 4-7)

Children more fully understand explanations, descriptions, rules, and suggestions of other regulations and participate in verbal discussions about tasks. This enables children to more correctly sense the demands of a task and enables them to choose what must be done to successfully perform. This stage is characterized by indications that children are beginning to defer gratification and develop impulse control.

Self-Regulation Assurance (Ages 8-12)

Children can now identify their strategies of self-regulation and adopt them or form new ones to fit different situations. Adapting them, however, involves checking for external or adult confirmation. One may see responses ranging from well-developed self-regulation to pronounced attempts to gain confirmation from others.

Self-Regulation (Ages 12-18)

Children's adaptive strategies can be clearly observed as they successfully participate in varieties of activities. Self-regulation is made definite in the forms of impulse control, resistance to temptation, and self-control. Adolescents formulate plans to perform tasks and achieve more of them by using strategies of self-regulation. ❀

A Practical
Identity

The word "identity" may be somewhat vague to you and in some ways it is not easy to understand. Yet, as a practical part of life, we all know many things about it and use this knowledge every day. For example, everyone can be identified by a name, religion, nationality, cultural background, career, and hobby. "I am a teacher," "I am from Peru," and "I am a hard worker," are examples of identity statements.

Identity is made up of the knowledge we possess about ourselves. This "self-knowledge" exists when we become aware of our inherited abilities and characteristics, such as height, weight, and other physical traits. In addition, we also acquire self-knowledge about ways we act, how we think, and what we feel. A person, for example, could know about her intellectual abilities and emotional style. She could know that she is loved and supported, or not loved and supported, by others. An identity is formed when this information is first discovered and then integrated in some organized way. When this takes place, the result is fairly permanent. Identity is not a shirt we put on and take off when it is convenient or when we feel like it. Identity is the meaning found in the words we use to describe ourselves and others. We talk about identity when we say, "I am a happy person," or "She is very loving," or "I trust him because he is honest."

The biological basis for identity exists in the structure of the brain, which develops and organizes our thoughts and experiences. As we grow and mature, our brains develop increased abilities to organize, synthesize, and integrate what we think and feel and how we act. This is natural. All people go through the same process. This is similar to what happens when we put a jigsaw puzzle together. While the pieces are in the box its identity is a puzzle. Even when we are putting the pieces together we think of it as a puzzle. But, when the very last piece is placed, or integrated, we think of it as a picture of some kind. The integration of all the parts has made the puzzle into a new concept or identity.

Importance of Identity

Identity is the most basic and far-reaching idea in human behavior. It is related to virtually everything we do. Since it is all that we think about when we think about ourselves, it comes into play in virtually every choice, every act, and every relationship. Our religious beliefs, our values, and our work behavior are all part of identity. It is motivation for performance and achievement. It is how we express ourselves as married people, parents, and friends.

Identity can also be understood from times when it is incomplete or not fully formed. Consider a child who has received frequent beatings from an overly harsh parent. These beatings take place whenever a parental rule has not been followed or when the parent acts without concern for the child. Since the beatings cause pain, the child begins to be afraid whenever there is concern about parental disapproval. What may happen as this child matures? It is possible that he will be more interested in avoiding the disapproval of others than becoming aware about himself and expressing his identity accurately. Limited self-knowledge prevents us from forming a complete sense of identity.

There are several conditions which prevent self-knowledge from emerging. These include excessive dependency between parent and child, emotional neglect of children by parents, early trauma, and enmeshment, a condition where a child is not permitted to form a sense of unique individuality. When one or more of these conditions exist, a developing child is prevented from acquiring self-knowledge. The pieces of his or her "life puzzle" cannot be put together, and the formation of identity is incomplete.

Signs of Complete and Incomplete Identity Formation

There are many indications of complete and incomplete identity formation. Life's problems are evidence that one's sense of identity is weak; life's successes exist when identity is strong.

Complete Identity Formation	Incomplete Identity Formation
more productive	less productive
strong sense of self-control	often depressed
satisfying relationships	unstable relationships
more positive emotions	more anxiety and anger
accepts responsibility	assumes too much guilt
assertive	inhibited

How To Maintain Identity

The pressures of routines and involvements in work, church, and relationships can weaken one's sense of identity. In order to feel secure and confident about what we do, it is necessary to learn maintenance skills which enable us to perpetuate a strong sense of identity. One of these is a sense of self-control. This is maintained by the awareness that we make choices that call for action and responsibility. Therefore, to maintain identity we need to have a procedure for making choices and accepting the results of our actions without blaming or criticizing anyone else for what happens. Secondly, identity is maintained by a condition of separation.

This means that instead of linking ourselves to others by suggesting they cause what we think, feel, or do, we need to attribute the cause of what we are to ourselves. This will sound like, "I do this because of what I think or feel," or "I think this because of what I feel," or "I feel this because I think this." This separating of our thoughts from the acts of other people will remove the false links we establish with other people. Third, maintaining a strong sense of identity is accomplished when we learn to be expressive. That is, to say what we think or feel in many different situations. When we are expressive we feel more positive than when we cannot speak about our own thoughts and feelings.

Imagine yourself going on a date, conversing with parents, talking with a church authority, deciding what to do with a friend, or arguing with a brother or sister. In which of these situations are you most likely to blame, feel your behavior is caused by someone else, or see yourself as inhibited? Your answers will tell you the situations in which you have the easiest and hardest times maintaining your sense of identity.   ❈

Identity Formation

Begun when children are very young and elaborated as they mature, the sense of individuality we call identity is more fully realized during the latter parts of adolescence and early adulthood. Identity formation within human beings is a combination of many things. Among these are the following: (1) goals and the ability to organize to reach them, (2) appropriate understanding of important social roles (e.g., husband, friend, wife, parent, etc.), (3) self-regulation, and (4) a capacity for fun and enjoyment.

Individuals develop these characteristics at varying rates, but there is some evidence (Montemayor & Eisen 1977) that all development follows some clearly discernable trends. These authors asked children of different ages to respond to the question, "Who am I?" Younger children answered by associating themselves with places, other people, and physical characteristics. Older children were more likely to think of themselves in abstract ways (e.g., "I am a good friend," or "I am a human being"). We can conclude from this report that much of the formation of identity is due to maturation of body and brain.

Like nearly all other areas of development, however, a positive identity is also due to conditions in one's environment. These conditions appear to be actual achievement, self-awareness, and self-regulation. A person could be said to use abstract thinking, achievements, knowledge about self, and the confidence acquired from self-control to organize attitudes which comprise the larger concept of identity. An individual who does not achieve, has little self-awareness, or fails to regulate behavior would have difficulty achieving a sense of identity.

Of interest to us, is the unique way an individual uses abstract thought to integrate maturational and environmental influences. During late adolescence, it seems the major activity in identity formation is the synthesizing of several parts of one's personality. One person may use achievement more prominently in the way identity is expressed while another may use some other aspect.

It seems clear that identity depends on an individual finding ways to see relationships between many characteristics which previously have been separate. These relationships may be similar to recognizing how one thinks or feels about many different people or situations and concluding that "I am generally optimistic," or "I think things over carefully before I decide." Adolescence may be characterized as the time when individuals integrate and develop a sense of "wholeness" about themselves.

Anyone wishing to contribute to the formation of another's identity can do so by helping the person first achieve self-awareness and self-control. Then, activities, including conversations and decision-making which require a synthesis of personality characteristics, can be used to promote an integration of this condition into a fairly stable sense of identity.

Development of Identity

Individual Status (Ages 0-3)

Environment: Learns and relates to a name. Acquires knowledge about the world and begins to adapt to people and the uses of objects.
Maturation: Development of senses, physical abilities, earliest sex-roles adjustment. Achieves physical skills of eating, toilet training, running, walking, and skipping.

Social Status (Ages 3-7)

Environment: The adaptation to varieties of social situations promotes self-knowledge in fairly concrete ways. "I can now run fast ... I am big!" These self-references are used as explanations for social status.

Maturation: Begins to use physical abilities as a primary way of relating to other people. Social status is based on how skillful or unskillful a child may be.

Achievement (Ages 7-12)

Environment: Children develop levels of achievement motivation and use them in various tasks. These may include academic work, specialized talents, and/or chores at home. The ability to utilize self-regulation comes into play in order to balance achievement activities with other experiences. Achievement becomes more specialized and individuals begin to better recognize what they might successfully achieve.

Maturation: Cognitive maturation allows the emotional control necessary in achievement behavior. Increased mental growth also permits more focused introspection that results in greater awareness of one's attitudes, motives, and moods.

Identity Formation (Ages 13 and older)

Environment: Increased social involvement promotes more awareness and self-consciousness. Achievements can be recognized by important groups and used to achieve status.

Maturation: Children show an improved ability to think abstractly, which permits them to perceive relationships among their own personality traits. These relationships are formed into the generalized beliefs that make up the concept of identity.   ❀

The Development
of Independence

Independence is a general concept widely used to describe a child's separation from parents, but there is little agreement about what it specifically means. It is usually viewed as financial self-sufficiency, and in a more abstract way, as emotional or psychological separation. Achieving it is viewed as a major developmental task of adolescence because independence is an indication of maturity.

Children who are independent are more likely to make individual decisions, feel able to rely on themselves for survival, and believe their efforts have reasonable chances of succeeding. Independent people are, according to Erikson's stages of development, better able to establish intimate relationships. The relationship of independent children to parents is one of equality and mutual respect. Children acknowledge the parents' position by deferring occasionally to parental involvement and parents show respect by seldom advising or otherwise intruding in their children's lives. Parents and independent children are able to strike a positive balance between affection and individuality.

How Adolescents Achieve Independence

Of the attempts to study how adolescents achieve independence, one stands out as especially significant. Daniel and Janet Offer collected information about their subjects over an eight-year period. Results from the study showed three avenues of achieving independence: 1. continuous growth (twenty-three percent of the total group), 2. surgent growth (thirty-five percent of the total group), and 3. tumultuous growth (twenty-one percent of the total group).

Those who experienced continuous growth coped well with internal and external stimuli and had mastered previous developmental stages without serious problems. Their parents grew and changed with them. There was open expression of affection between parents and children during the eight years and capacity was exhibited to delay gratification and work for a future goal. Further, children expressed emotions but seldom let the expression get out of control.

Individuals in the group of surgent growth appeared to experience rapid personality change and achieve independence in a short time period. These individuals showed reasonable coping behavior, but when a crisis arose, they tended to become angry and blame others. Consequently, relationships between adolescents and parents were not smooth. Furthermore, the parents of these individuals evidenced conflict between their basic values. These subjects were not as action-oriented as the first group and were late in developing heterosexual interests. They were less able to be introspective than the others and evidenced constricted emotional responses.

Individuals who experienced tumultuous growth came from less favorable backgrounds than individuals in the other two groups. Many parents had open marital conflict and others had histories of mental illness. Parents appeared to be unsure of their values and failed to present clearly-defined values to their children. Both parents and children had difficulty separating from one another and their relationships were marked by great emotional intensity. Independence was achieved after years of instability and conflict.

The results of this study show that at least three avenues of independence exist. Further, we can see the close tie between the course of independence and a child's background. When we consider that mental and physical development are antecedents to independence, we can begin to recognize the complexity involved.

How To Promote Independence

Being independent is considered important by our culture. Because it is, those who achieve it benefit from the reinforcement and respect given by others. Those who have difficulty achieving independence from parents receive less admiration. Those who are involved with children and hope for their success can contribute by knowing how to help them prepare for increased independence.

Independence is promoted when children have stable families and positive relationships with parents. Beyond this, however, there are more specific things which promote independence. One of these is ensuring that children, while young, have work of their own to perform and learn to do it responsibly. Early development of a sense of achievement and responsibility for tasks is usually formed when children have regular household chores to perform or other outside activities like paper routes or achievement in school or sports.

Further, as children mature they can be helped to become more independent by being helped to make and carry out decisions regarding their own activities. One set of parents asked their children to participate in making decisions about homework, curfew time, and chores. Further, the parents frequently asked their children's opinions about values and current affairs. When the children's opinions differed markedly from the parents, further conversations were invited. This joint participation was marked by encouragement from the parents. Plans about children's future activities away from home such as work or school were also talked about. Achieving independence seemed natural and appropriate.

Another set of parents decided their children should be independent by age eighteen. Working backwards from that time, they selected several events that children would do in gradual stages and specified awards for doing them. They worked out contracts with their children and reported that children responded well to their plan.

The many different circumstances of life for young adults make the setting of the same effective procedures impossible for each person. It is likely better to understand some principles and guidelines and then apply them to children in an individual way. Some increased freedom, gradually reduced controls, well-defined values, positive support, and a history of responsible achievement appear to be the ingredients necessary to achieve independence from parents.

The Development of Independence

Sense of Self (Ages 0-11)

Children emerge as individuals by developing age-adequate language, physical, cognitive, and social skills. A sense of self happens through early achievement, social experiences, and participation in family interaction.

Controlled (Ages 12-15)

This stage consists of membership in peer groups and greater social involvement. Separation permits children to explore a wider range of experiences within a relatively secure environment. Children begin to exhibit "negative compliance," or opposition to the rules or values of authority figures. Mild negative compliance is usually viewed as a more positive predictor of independence. Extreme opposition, passive or aggressive, indicates a lack of progress toward independence.

Individuation (Ages 16-22)

Children further refine individual opinions, values, and behavioral standards usually similar to their parents. Children may apply them in highly-unique ways. Authority figures lose much of their image as rule givers and are viewed by children more realistically possessing ordinary human characteristics. Children also have developed future plans and are progressing toward them.   ❀

Dating and Courtship

Dating and courtship are the terms our society uses to describe the way adolescents become acquainted with heterosexual partners and establish intimate bonds. What people actually do to accomplish this is usually determined by the culture in which they live. In the United States, young people generally engage in courtship with more freedom to choose partners and activities than youth in Far Eastern countries, whose parents often select the partners and choose the courtship activities.

Although the patterns of dating and courtship are strongly influenced by an individual's cultural heritage, they are approached by young people in a developmental way. There appear to be some phases of dating and courting that are gradually entered into and which progress toward the culminating intimate relationship. Knowledge of these stages of growth enables us to consider what might be done to influence and improve the quality of this important social experience.

Early adolescents, recognizing considerable individual variation, usually begin to associate with members of the opposite sex for the purposes of being liked by others, acquiring a sense of self-esteem from the social contact, and participating with peers in group activities. Dating takes the form of heterosexual group activities that take place in a "friendship" atmosphere. "Hanging out" at a popular cafe or other setting is a frequent past time for adolescents who are entering into dating and courting relationships. These situations tend to be more relaxed and are more comfortable because they put less pressure on youth to participate in the emotional complexity of a "couple" relationship. These group contacts serve the purpose of teaching adolescents about how to meet other people, how to talk, and the general procedure of carrying out a "date."

When couple dating begins at about fourteen to seventeen years of age, adolescents enter into a period of mixed accomplishments. In the earlier parts of this period, dating takes place for the purpose of achieving or maintaining popularity. This dating reinforces some behavior which may not be linked to the emotional qualities of a good spouse or a good partner. The best dates, according to the adolescents, are often those who can talk freely and keep things going, usually at a superficial level. Further, since dating is an indicator of popularity, not being involved is viewed as so negative that adolescents develop manipulative interpersonal games that are contrary to the formation of a more genuine intimacy.

Following this second phase of the dating and courtship process, adolescents begin to date as a means of learning about one another and to find enjoyable heterosexual companionship. This leads to a more authentic and emotionally intense relationship that leads some to marriage. Others go through the pangs of fluctuating involvements, eventually going on to other experiences.

The last phase of dating and courtship is more properly called courting because its purpose is mate selection. Individuals date and enter into relationships to find compatibility leading to marriage. Lengthy conversations and a variety of explorations reveal information that serves the purpose of deciding on a mate.

Applying What We Know about Dating and Courtship

There are at least two ways we can apply what we know about dating and courtship. One is to evaluate ourselves and our abilities according to the developmental phases described in the previous section.

Another application is in the preparation of adolescents who are about to experience or who are currently involved in the dating process. Accurate information can help us make choices that contribute to our success.

When you evaluate yourself you can examine your recent dating experiences to find the phase or stage you are currently involved in. You can also identify the level of personal dating skills you have developed to this point and see if you are preparing yourself to progress.

You might also prepare yourself to use the information about dating and courtship to help others make good choices about what they can do to have enjoyable dating experiences. Your future children, your friends, or your younger brothers and sisters might be helped by what you can tell them.

Developmental Stages for Dating and Courtship

Early Adolescence

Getting Acquainted: Adolescents form groups of heterosexual friends. These groups meet at school, church, or a favorite community location (e.g., drive-in cafe) to talk and learn the preliminary dating skills.

Middle Adolescence

Dating for Status: Dating is often for the purpose of maintaining social status or to achieve a certain level of popularity with same sex friends. Dating is often accompanied by superficial forms of interpersonal behavior. These may include attempts at sexual exploration.

Middle to Late Adolescence

Dating for Companionship: Increased social and personal confidence allows progress toward selecting people to date that provide enjoyment and satisfying companionship. Individuals communicate more authentically and attempts are made to identify mutual interests. Individuals now have enough knowledge to observe and evaluate their personality characteristics and those of their companions.

Late Adolescence to Adulthood

Mate Selection: Dating loses some of its early casualness and becomes the method of exploring for and selecting a marriage partner. Interpersonal skills are refined and used to gather information enabling individuals to decide whether or not to marry. The style of communication includes many personal references and mutual evaluations of interpersonal dynamics. ❀

Delinquency

An individual is labeled delinquent because development is not taking place toward the conventional values of society. Such delinquency is usually indicated by the expression of behavior considered deviant by those who follow society's rules.

Individuals who perform deviant acts and betray the values of society or their families have developed this behavior much like development which takes place in other personality areas. Delinquent individuals include those who merely experiment with acts like shoplifting, drug usage, or deception, as well as those who participate with peer groups in more regular deviant acts.

A careful analysis suggests that deviant actions symbolize the areas in which growth has not taken place. Sometimes we focus so much attention on finding ways to prevent deviance that we fail to consider an equally important idea. What prevents or hinders positive or conventional development from taking place? A consideration of this question may lead us to understand that delinquency, like positive growth, has its own developmental characteristics.

The roots of delinquency are probably related to any delay of ordinary development. Late physical development may be a factor. Social isolation in some form may also contribute. Parental neglect, which may hinder social development, and parental over-protection, which hinders growth of a sense of responsibility, may also be involved. A child's own temperament may lead to social difficulty and experimentation with deviant acts. These children usually make friends who are similar in their values and level of maturity. These friendships often exert such great influence that parents and other authorities find themselves in a position weakened by peer pressure. Sometimes children cannot be influenced and delinquent behavior runs the full course until some external influence or maturity helps them live more closely to the conventional rules of society.

When delinquent children are influenced toward increased maturity, it is largely because the underlying reasons for the behavior have been identified and responded to correctly. A child may be delinquent in developing because of some emotional trauma such as parental divorce or death. In this case, resolution of the unfulfilled emotional need through discussion and love may be required. Other children may be delinquent because of a slow maturation rate. These children require guidance, support, and patience. Other children become caught in the web of environmental events and, in order to grow, must change their circumstances or be removed from them. The best strategy, however, is not to overreact but to accumulate as much information as possible about the child and then choose a course of action based on the reasons for the delinquent behavior.

The Development of Delinquency

The Diminished Self (Ages 0-10)

Children, by virtue of neglect, overprotection, emotional enmeshment, delayed maturation, and/or abuse are prevented from developing a strong sense of individuality. They may manifest dependent behavior on parents, extreme temperament shifts, learning disorders, and/or problems relating to friends.

Experimental (Ages 11-13)

Delinquent children begin to experiment with and engage in activities which are precisely opposite of those desired by authority figures (e.g., if parents want the child to succeed in school he or she will fail). This is called negative compliance. Children show a greater tendency to lie and deceive as a means of creating a sense of increased freedom. This is an illusion. Experiments with deviant acts usually involve sensual activities such as drugs, alcohol, or sexual experiences.

Delinquent Peer Groups (Ages 14 and older)

Delinquent children join with other delinquent children and participate in deviant acts as a group. Group membership supports the children against guilt and/or pressure placed on them by authority figures. Group activities become central to their thinking and participation in deviant experiences is a requirement for membership. Values about personal responsibility, relationship to authority, and religious beliefs are mirrored among group members. ❀

Sex Roles

Sex roles pervade every aspect of life. In every culture men and women have different duties, responsibilities, chores, and tasks. Sex roles are the socially prescribed ways a culture defines behavior of the different genders. Since there are vast differences in the sex roles that societies assign their members, we know that sex roles are learned and are not inherent in the nature of maleness or femaleness.

Gender typing (the awareness of one's gender) occurs in the early pre-school years. It seems to involve two processes. There is the process of learning which gender a person is and learning what a person of that gender is supposed to do. As children begin to comprehend themselves and their world, one of the first things they understand, or concepts they form, is their own gender. They identify themselves as male or female and begin to organize their roles on the basis of that awareness. Once a child's understanding of gender is firmly established, for example, a boy knows he is a boy, he begins to use members of his own sex as models for his behavior. Children form concepts of what boys and girls should be like. Then, their concepts broaden and stretch. For instance, a girl may realize that short hair does not necessarily mean that someone is a boy as she comes in contact with boys and men who have long hair and women who have short hair.

Eventually, the child's own self-concept becomes assimilated into the concept of gender (i.e., "I am a female, thus the qualities I possess are qualities of femaleness."). At this point, children have a feedback loop. They compare their behaviors and actions with their concepts of maleness and femaleness, and then they evaluate themselves. This acts as a motivation to help them conform their behaviors to the concept of their gender that they have developed.

Parents play an important role in helping a child develop a concept of gender. In families where parents have traditional views of male and female roles, a child will also develop that same concept. An interesting topic in developmental psychology today is the question of whether there should be specific gender roles for men and women. Sandra Bem has suggested that human behaviors and personality attributes should not be linked to gender. Instead of the stereotypical notions of masculinity and femininity, a concept has evolved of "androgyny." An androgynous person is one who describes himself or herself with both traditionally masculine adjectives and traditionally feminine adjectives. Since androgynous people score high in both masculine and feminine kinds of traits, we might expect them to be the optimal functioning human beings. Indeed, some research has shown that people with high self-esteem score high on an androgyny test. Androgynous people are very flexible in their roles and can adapt to whatever role their present situations in life demand. They do not see the world in terms of specific tasks assigned to men and women, but see a blending of tasks and shared responsibility.

In college "Preparation for Marriage" classes, the vast majority of students claim they would like to have a companionate marriage (one where both partners share jobs equally). Sometimes the wife cooks and cleans up, and sometimes the husband. Sometimes the husband takes care of the children, and sometimes the wife. The distribution of duties is determined by the individual needs and free time of each individual partner. The kind of personality that lends itself most ideally to a companionate marriage is the androgynous personality.

It should be noted that a marriage between two androgynous people is not the only successful kind of marriage. An excellent marriage can be made between a very traditional masculine male and feminine female because there is a clear understanding of the roles of each partner.

Androgynous people differ from traditionally masculine and feminine people in their beliefs about the differences between the sexes. Androgynous people see very few psychological differences between the sexes. They see that there are more intra-sex differences on any psychological trait than there are inter-sex differences. The trend among college age students seems to be toward an equality and a fuzzing of the line between male and female roles.

Given the barrage of gender-related information that children encounter on television, in advertising, and with toys, how can a parent help a child to develop an androgynous personality? One way is for parents to make gender irrelevant in the home. Activities such as who cooks and does dishes, what toys are available, what games children can play, and what roles children can pick when they play house should not be determined by a child's sex.

When their children are young, parents can select books and television programs which teach children that one's sex is mostly a matter of anatomical differences and reproductive traits and not much else. They can point out examples of members of both sexes doing wide varieties of tasks and being happy, content, and fulfilled in doing them.

When androgynous college men were asked about their families, they said that their fathers had been highly involved in their lives and that they felt close to their mothers. Similarly, androgynous women tended to be close to their fathers and had mothers who modeled and encouraged achievement in intellectual pursuits, curiosity, and schoolwork.

It is unlikely that society will abolish or reverse gender roles totally. This is sad in some ways because many obstacles to the advancement of women are based upon the prejudices or preconceived notions that others have of what women should do.

Remember that an androgynous person is no better or worse than a person with more traditional concepts of gender. It does seem important for a person to become aware of his or her beliefs about sex roles and have tolerance for others' beliefs. It also seems wise that for an androgynous person to marry another androgynous person because they will have similar expectations of each other. ❀

Interpersonal Reasoning

Thinking about yourself in relationship to another person is called interpersonal reasoning. The ability to be successful at it implies that we reason well about ourselves and understand how our thoughts and feelings might be similar or dissimilar to those of other people. This competence permits us to observe our behavior and others' behavior as part of a relationship experience.

Not everyone is equally skillful at interpersonal reasoning. But some skill appears, on the surface, to be a part of all satisfying relationships. Likewise, inadequacy to reason well may contribute to diminished satisfaction.

The development of interpersonal reasoning appears to depend in part on the use of language. When parents use "I-you" language (e.g., "I love you" and "It seems to me you are unhappy"), children learn to use it as part of their routine verbal expression. Early words and behavioral references for the words then allow an individual to gradually expand vocabulary and improve and refine observational skills.

Being able to gather observations about interpersonal behavior enables us to infer what one's actions may mean. After observing someone's facial expression and vocal tone, we could say and infer something about that person's feelings which we cannot directly see. When we infer or guess correctly, our judgments are reinforced and we feel more adequate to predict other interpersonal events. Those capable of observing and inferring the most accurately about themselves and others will usually find greater reward in social experiences. Misjudgment resulting from inadequate observations and inaccurate inferences obviously may lead to increased conflict and dissatisfaction.

One can readily understand why interpersonal reasoning is closely tied to any given language culture. We use words to symbolize observable and unobservable interpersonal events. Most of us know and appreciate that words of one language do not literally translate to words of another. The subtleties of the words in any language often cannot be accurately understood before one has had extensive practice.

The expression of love, for example, is an interpersonal event. Yet, how it is expressed and observed might differ from person to person because of different experiences.

How We Can Influence the Development of Interpersonal Reasoning

Children can benefit from any focused attempt to enrich their learning. Parents can enhance children's abilities to reason interpersonally by increasing the amount of time they think and learn about the social world. When children are participants in varieties of social experiences and have discussed opportunities about them, they can observe more accurately. When these are tested and reinforced, skill increases as they anticipate future rewards.

Other effective ways children learn to reason about interpersonal behavior is through imitation, games, and social play. These activities allow practice in a more secure situation. The true-to-life imitations sharpen observational skills and improve the inferences children can make about them.

Stages of Development

The Proving Age: (Ages 0-6)

Children gather information from the family and other social environments. Preliminary tests are made to learn which assumption can be relied on.

Their ability to make inferences about social conditions is limited by the amount of experience and children's sense of egocentrism.

Social Inferences (Ages 7-12)

At age six, children can infer that someone's thoughts might differ from their own. By age eight, children know that others can understand them. By age ten, children can distinguish what others think from what they think.

Refinement (Ages 13 and older)

Increased varieties of social experience and attempts to validate what is observed leads to a continual refinement of interpersonal reasoning. Individuals begin to apply their reasoning skills to specific areas of interest and need such as heterosexual relationships and work environments. ❀

Development of Adolescent Peer Groups

No study of adolescence in American society would be complete without understanding the development of adolescent peer groups. Membership in peer groups is part of nearly everyone's experience during adolescence and often exerts great influence on us.

The basis for peer groups is probably the social and emotional need to take a small step away from home-like conditions and establish an identity with same-age individuals. Most adolescents have similar emotional and social needs which provide the motivation for them to join together as a means of finding satisfaction. By studying adolescent peer groups we can increase our understanding of the adolescent period of life.

There are three general stages of group membership that adolescents create: same sex groups, heterosexual groups, and dating pairs. Youth think about an abstract group which serves as an "audience" for their social behavior. Parents know this group by the name of "they." A teen may say, "They are all going," or "They are wearing this style of clothing." Youth also join groups that serve as "models" for them to emulate and which critically evaluate their performance.

All social groups have rules of membership and exert pressure for individuals to comply with them. These may be informal or formal and include such things as style of dress, use of new vocabulary, loyalty oaths, and time involvement. Failure to satisfy these rules may result in an individual being excluded. Since acceptance usually is a strong motive, the threat of exclusion often places an individual under considerable amounts of pressure to comply. This is one of the reasons why peer groups exert great influence on adolescents.

The composition of peer groups and the types of participation change as children mature and become more socially aware. Same-sex groups are the first to form. Members come together to serve a common task or because they are in similar geographical locations. This first stage is followed by membership in groups which allow individuals to perform social

tasks such as meet members of the other sex and promote status in the larger social networks of school,
church, and community. Heterosexual groups form in
the next stage when higher status members begin to
date. Generally, members of these groups have similar
socio-economic backgrounds and are organized
according to levels of status in their community. The
last stage of peer groups consists of dating pairs who
balance time between dating alone and with other
member pairs. Eventually time and commitment to
the group wanes and couples spend more time on
their own.

How Group Membership Helps Children Develop

Peer groups are the chief means by which children are helped to move away from parental ties and
achieve independence. In our society they provide
opportunities for individuals to gradually participate
in society. Group membership gives individuals
opportunities to gather information about themselves
which can be used to promote one's identity.

Because these two useful purposes are accomplished by group membership, parents and others
involved with child care can ensure that children have
a positive experience. More open and free communication with parents can help children select groups that
provide fun and positive social experiences. Parents
can, for example, become acquainted with their own
children's friends and communicate support for them

to be together. This may also require parents to adjust family rules to allow for increased flexibility. Rather than fear those changes in the family, parents can view them as part of the process which eventually will result in their children's independence. Further, parents can engage their children in formulating steps toward increased independence and place themselves in positions of support rather than of indifference and restriction.

It is well-known, of course, that many parents find their adolescent children in peer groups that do not reflect family values. This is made more likely by the presence of conflict in the home and by weak family ties. When this situation exists, it presents difficulty for all involved. The adolescent, however, is usually the person who is most adversely affected because he or she is the one developing and changing. Conflict between parents and children that involves peers is unsettling and disruptive at this time in life when important developmental tasks could be accomplished. Conflict can delay personality development and alter its form. Adolescents should be informed of the importance group selection can have for them. ❀

Achievement Motivation

Unless impaired in some way, all infants show a remarkable motivation to learn and improve. It is expressed in the intense efforts infants make to creep, crawl, walk, and run. All physical, social, and psychological development during infancy can be traced in part to this motivation.

Since motivation is present in virtually every young child, it is reasonable that children would apply it to achievement in areas other than developmental tasks. These may include improvement of talents, academic performance, and some social skills. Behavioral scientists have labeled this motivation as achievement motivation.

After infancy, this motivation is not present in all children to the same degree. It seems reasonable to assume that some events or experiences must have taken place to inhibit the expression of achievement motivation. It may also be the case that the original sense of competency received such little reinforcement that other adaptations were learned.

The literature describing the development of achievement motivation clearly and consistently suggests that it is the result of individuals, such as parents or older siblings, and social environments, such as play groups or school, actively promoting it (McClelland 1955; DeCharms and Moeller 1962).

This means that achievement motivation is the result of a child's actions combined with what parents, school teachers, and other acquaintances might contribute. When this is not accomplished, children are said to develop a fear of failure, which on the surface appears to be somewhat like achievement motivation, but as we shall see, is quite different.

Achievement motivation is characterized by positive attitudes about the task, moderate amounts of tension, clear belief that the person can succeed at the task, organized efforts, and persistence to completion of the task. Fear of failure is, in contrast to achievement motivation, characterized by an extreme intensity about a task or by passivity. Further, tasks are faced with apprehension and a genuine fear that failure, not success, will take place. In extreme cases, fear of failure is so intense that performance is impaired. An example is test anxiety which reduces students' levels of performance because of the mental blocks it creates.

How To Develop Achievement Motivation

Learning to achieve requires two mental abilities: the ability to organize and define success and the ability to maintain energy levels high enough to impel action and low enough to permit an adequate response. Defining success is learned when children are shown exactly what to do, encouraged to do well, and rewarded when the task is complete. When this sequence is repeated many times throughout childhood, it becomes an individual's way of approaching any performance.

Interestingly, this sequence is learned more effectively when a child is started on a task and supervised in alternating sequences. As children mature, external rewards are supplanted by the satisfaction that stems from doing what is predicted. True achievement motivation is predicting the level of performance and then achieving it.

The ability to regulate energy, or the arousal part of achievement motivation, is both learned and based on inherited characteristics. Children appear to reduce high arousal and increase low arousal. Apparently, everyone has an individual range of energy that contributes to optimal performance. This tendency seems to appear in all primates, suggesting it is inherited.

The actual range of variation, however, seems to be affected by learning. A child reared in a calm environment may have a different range of optimal arousal than one who has experienced excessive amounts of extreme emotions. Ironically, the experience of extreme emotions tends to reduce the optimal energy range.

The role of learning in achievement motivation stems largely from the types of activities children are taught to use in reducing or increasing arousal. As part of child care, for example, parents may put a child on a chair or in an isolated situation to reduce arousal. Children can use an inner dialogue to alter emotional states. The presence of other people, either in cooperation or as an audience, may affect arousal levels. Children may learn to anticipate a reward for performing if consequences are positive, or they may feel guilt if consequences are too punitive. Positive consequences, over time, yield a less extreme range of arousal, while guilt from punitive consequences tends to create arousal so extreme that performance levels are reduced. This is the aforementioned condition termed fear of failure.

Development of Achievement Motivation

Arousal Reduction (Ages 0-2)

After birth, children seek arousal-reducing activities. Until the age of two, achievement is a result of maturation and reflexive responses including motor activities and cognitive growth.

Arousal Increase and Exploration (Ages 3-6)

Children begin to increase arousal by exploring more and satisfying curiosity drive. Arousal levels begin to be randomly tied to satisfaction of discovery and performance.

Integration of Arousal and Performance (Ages 7-12)

Children tie performance tasks to strategies of reducing and increasing arousal. School, chores at home, and social events are sources of learning. Positive or punitive reactions of other people to children's performance influence children's arousal levels. Encouragement and rewards lead to higher levels of achievement motivation.

Performance and Prediction (Ages 13-18)

Children further refine achievement motivation by developing predictions about their performance. Those high in achievement motivation take intermediate risks and adjust downward on second attempts if they fail on first efforts. Those low in achievement motivation either take no risks or excessive risks. Failure is responded to by an exaggerated prediction, usually upward from previous predictions. Failure produces increased arousal, and children believe they must do more on subsequent attempts to compensate for the first failure. These characteristics become highly stylized, and long-term traits appear to be established.   ❈

Prenatal
Development

Child development begins at conception. In fact, the time between conception and birth is the most dynamic period of an individual's existence. This period of prenatal development begins when a man's sperm fertilizes a woman's egg and ends when the child is born. Much of a child's future hinges on what happens during prenatal development. From the very beginning, when the sperm and egg meet, certain things are already determined. What color a child's hair, eyes, and skin will be, for example, is informed by the genetic information contained within the sperm and egg. Current research in the field of behavior genetics is also investigating the link between our genes and traits such as intelligence, personality, and mental illness. Other things are also determined upon conception. Birth defects, for example, are often the result of problems with our genetic material. As development continues, environmental factors influence a child's potential development after birth. Each moment during prenatal development brings change and growth. A mother's behavior and her environment can affect the growing baby inside her which will often determine the development of the child after birth. A basic explanation of the stages of prenatal development will make this idea more understandable.

The development of the baby is continuous, but growth can be easily described according to trimesters. The first trimester includes months one through three; the second trimester includes months four through six; the third trimester includes months seven through nine, ending with the birth of the baby. During each trimester, different characteristics and organs of the baby develop.

The First Trimester

When the man's sperm fertilizes the woman's egg, a zygote is formed. During the first two weeks following fertilization, the zygote's cells divide rapidly, and the zygote implants itself in the uterine wall. If implantation is successful, the embryo begins to form. The embryo begins to develop differentiated cells, such as those for the heart, muscles, bones, skin, and reproductive system. Within weeks, the embryo has developed distinguishable legs, arms and facial features. When eight weeks have passed, the embryo becomes a fetus. A fetus looks essentially human, although it still must undergo great development.

By the end of the first trimester, the baby weighs about half an ounce. The umbilical cord, which attaches the fetus to the mother, has been circulating blood between the baby and the uterine wall. The umbilical cord is soft but very strong. This is how the fetus receives oxygen. The placenta has also begun to function. The fetus receives nourishment and excretes wastes by the placenta, and the placenta is responsible for the fetus' growth. Waste products from the fetus are filtered through the placenta into the mother's bloodstream so she can excrete them for the fetus.

The placenta is fully formed by the end of the first trimester and acts like a filter for oxygen, food, and antibodies from the mother to the fetus. Protecting the fetus is a sack of amniotic fluid. This fluid is constantly being made by the mother's body and contains salt and nutrients that the fetus absorbs through its skin. Amniotic fluid also contains many minerals, sugar, skin cells from the fetus, pieces of vernix (waxy coating on the fetus), and products of fetal urine.

By the end of the third month, the fetus' muscles begin to respond to signals sent by the brain. Many physical details are taking place, including the development of taste buds, production of saliva, and the development of vocal cords and tooth buds for baby teeth. The eyes begin to move closer to the center of the face and the nose is present. The head becomes more proportionate to the rest of the body. The limbs, hands and feet are growing very rapidly. External reproductive organs are continuing to develop and are becoming recognizable. All the essential organs have formed and are beginning to function. The liver is producing bile, the heart is pumping blood throughout the body, and the kidneys are fully developed as well.

The tremendous amount of development occurring during the first trimester makes it a very crucial time. Often problems with the heart, limbs, eyes, ears, palate, teeth, external genitalia, and brain experienced by an infant or young child can be traced to certain activities of the mother or environmental factors the fetus was exposed to during the first few months of prenatal development. These factors, called teratogens, are known causes of birth defects. These will be discussed shortly.

The Second Trimester

During the second trimester, the fetus experiences less dramatic growth, but important changes do occur. The fetus' movements can be felt by the mother, and the fetus responds to various stimulation. The fetus adopts some cycles of behavior such as waking and sleeping, and becomes more coordinated in its movements. It can stretch, yawn, suck its thumb, and even make facial expressions.

The baby is approximately thirteen inches long and 1 lb., 2 oz. by the end of the sixth month of pregnancy. During this trimester, lanugo, or a fine, downy hair, begins to develop all over the baby's body. Body fat accumulates to prepare the fetus for birth and the change of environment birth will bring. By the end of the second trimester, external genital organs are developed enough to be able to tell the sex of the baby by using an ultrasound. If the baby is a girl, her internal reproductive organs are also formed. The limbs are fully developed and the fetus can move all joints. The fetus has grown hair, eyebrows and eyelashes.

The fetus' body has also started producing white blood cells. These cells help fight off disease and infection. The hearing system is fully developed. Fingerprints and toeprints are visible, and the skin becomes opaque. The tongue is now fully developed. Also, by the end of this trimester, the heartbeat can be heard through a stethoscope. The parts of the body most sensitive to defects at this time are the eyes, teeth, external genitalia, and the central nervous system.

The Third Trimester

The most significant changes during the third trimester include growth in the fetus' length and weight, as well as continued brain development. At the end of the third trimester, or at the time of birth, the baby is usually anywhere from six to eleven pounds. The average newborn baby is seven-and-a-half pounds and twenty inches long. The fetus continues to develop more fat under the skin in order to regulate its own body temperature at birth. Throughout the third trimester, the placenta begins to diminish, and the amount of amniotic fluid decreases as the fetus continues to grow.

All organs except the lungs are fully developed by the end of the third trimester. The air sacs inside the lungs make surfactant, which is a liquid to prevent the baby's lungs from collapsing when taking the first breath outside the womb. The brain has been steadily developing, which stimulates the operation of behavioral systems. Hearing is very well-developed, and many studies have been done to determine whether or not prenatal exposure to sounds affects later development.

The baby does respond to the sound of the mother's voice and rhythmic sounds resembling a heart beat. The fetus continues to be sensitive to the possibility of defects in the eyes, teeth, external genitalia, and central nervous system. Overall, if every stage of prenatal development has gone well, by the end of this final trimester the baby is fully developed. The baby will often turn to a vertex position (head down), and the head may drop into the mother's pelvis (engagement). The baby is in the position ready for birth.

The Effects of Environment on Prenatal Development

Prenatal development is an incredibly sensitive time. Unlike the beliefs of some, the womb is not a wholly protected and safe environment for the developing baby. While the uterus does provide protection from some outside influences, many of the environmental aspects a mother is in contact with simultaneously affect the growing fetus. In fact, some things which benefit a grown adult actually do significant damage in the prenatal stage.

Teratogens, or known causes of birth defects, can be divided into four categories. The first category is medical drugs. Many drugs prescribed to adults can cause severe birth defects, both physical and mental. The second category, maternal illnesses, likewise affect the developing fetus. Additional drugs, such as alcohol, tobacco, caffeine, and cocaine, have significant effects as well. Other things in a mother's environment can also affect the fetus such as lead or radiation. These teratogens usually cause severe problems, including deformities and mental retardation.

Studies also look at maternal characteristics which affect prenatal development. A mother's nutrition, age, and emotional well-being can put an infant at risk for experiencing developmental problems. Common problems include low birth weight and poor brain development. Some of these babies are born prematurely, experience mental retardation and physical handicaps, and have increased risk for infant mortality.

Birth complications can also affect a child's future development. One possibility, for example, is that the baby's oxygen supply is limited, potentially damaging organs and causing brain problems. Other problems occur when an infant is born prematurely or has a low birth weight, because the organs have not had the time to fully develop and the baby is susceptible to various impairments.

Potential parents may be overwhelmed by the risks involved during prenatal development. On a positive note, parents can do much to ensure their infant will enjoy good health and normal development simply by avoiding exposure to the various teratogens named above. It is also significant that studies have shown prenatal development is not the final determinant of a child's future success and development. Many of the physical problems can be corrected through surgery. Mental delays can be remedied through careful parenting. A child's environment can do much to reduce the effects of prenatal exposure to teratogens. Studies have shown that family stability, for example, highly increases the chances of normal development through life in spite of birth complications.

Findings such as these have particular implications. Obviously, knowledge of prenatal development will help parents make wise choices which will give their future child a head start. Equally important, knowledge of child development in general will help parents give their children a positive environment. This positive environment will do much with regards to stimulating growth and development in every stage of life. ❀

Physical Milestones: Birth to Two

A common phrase heard from parents of young children is, "Isn't it amazing how quickly they grow up? It seems like just yesterday when ..." Yes, infants and toddlers do grow at an astonishing rate. Infants, for example, usually triple their birth weight by the time they reach one year of age, which rate slows as they get older. Young children are constantly learning new things, and they seem to persistently beg us to teach them and expose them to more. The world is a brand new place to them, and their increasing physical abilities enable them to try new things, explore their environment, and experiment with using their bodies.

The stage from birth to age two is an amazing time with tremendous milestones of growth and development. As you watch your child advance through this period, you may be afraid to blink, not wanting to risk missing a crucial step. Understanding some of the major steps infants and toddlers go through will help you be aware of what to expect and how each of these steps influences future development. As you read through these steps, please be aware that all children develop at different rates. Rapid or delayed development are not sole indications of superiority or of problems. Also, keep in mind the following six concepts:

1. Physical development is tied to every other form of child development.

2. Physical development can be used as a barometer to measure successful development in other areas. In other words, if a child is consistently reaching physical milestones later than average, this might be an indication that there are other developmental problems.

3. Physical abilities are used for different purposes at different stages.

4. As children get older, they first use their physical abilities as a means of social participation. Toddlers and young children learn to play together and interact.

5. During middle childhood, children use their physical development as a means of social status. For example, the kids in elementary school who can run the fastest or bounce a ball the best are the most popular.

6. As puberty approaches, physical development translates into body image, which can have significant consequences in the lives of adolescents. Anorexia, for example, is a consequence of many girls and some boys becoming engrossed in how their bodies look.

Physical Growth

As was noted before, infants and toddlers grow very rapidly. Weight and height increase quickly. Boys are generally taller and heavier than girls, and differences are observed between the sizes of children from different races. As your baby grows, the proportions of the body will change. Newborns have very large heads and chests in proportion to the rest of their bodies. During the first two years, the lower half of the body makes significant gains while the torso and head grow at a slower rate. Hands and feet also grow slower than arms and legs.

Young children change physically in other ways as well. After birth, babies accumulate a great deal of fat, which continues until about nine months of age. After this point, the toddler discontinues storing this "baby fat," and you will notice a two year old is much slimmer than a baby. Babies lack much strength or physical coordination, which develop slowly as the child grows. A baby's skull, which is very soft at birth to facilitate movement through the birth canal, grows rapidly and hardens during the first two years. Teeth make their appearance, usually beginning at about six months, and two year olds have twenty teeth.

Brain Development

The rapid skull growth during the first two years reflects the great increases in brain size during this time. This growth is attributed to myelinization, or the process of maximizing the paths by which messages are sent through the brain. Also in the first two years of life, children's brains develop overwhelming numbers of connections where messages can be sent from one part of the brain to another.

Different parts of the brain develop at different times. Parts of the brain responsible for control of the head, arms, and chest develop before the parts controlling the legs. The last part of the brain to develop is the part responsible for consciousness and thought, which doesn't function very completely until about two years of age but continues in development for years into adulthood.

Most of us have heard of people being either right brained or left brained. During the first few years, the brain begins to specialize the right and left hemispheres. Specific tasks are usually controlled by one side or the other, but during the early years the brain seems able to adapt to damage by allowing the opposite hemisphere to take over control of the other's functions. The brain's ability to do so decreases rapidly over time, but its specialization continues for years to come.

Motor Development

Many parents anticipate the time when their infants will begin to develop coordination and strength. Milestones such as rolling over, sitting up, crawling, and standing are encouraged, praised, and documented. Motor development can be divided into two categories. Gross motor development includes movements which move the infant around like crawling or rolling over. Fine motor development includes smaller movements like picking things up and reaching for things. Motor development follows the growth patterns of the body. Control over the head develops first, followed by control of the torso and arms, and ending with control of the legs.

Stages of development are not isolated events. Rather, each new skill and area of control builds on a previous one. The chart on pages 292-293 presents a general schedule of when babies and toddlers gain certain motor skills. Keep in mind that great individual variation exists in development of these skills, but you may have cause for concern if your child consistently develops slowly in several of the following areas.

AGE	DEVELOPMENTAL SKILL
6 weeks	Holds head erect and steady
2 months	Lifts head and torso when lying on stomach Rolls from side to back
3-4 months	Grasps hand-size objects purposely
4 months	Rolls from back to side
7 months	Sits without help Crawls
8 months	Pulls self up to stand
9-10 months	Plays hand games like patty cake
11 months	Stands without help
11-12 months	Walks without help
12 months	Picks things up with pointer finger and thumb
13-14 months	Stacks objects
14 months	Scribbles

AGE	DEVELOPMENTAL SKILL
16 months	Ascends stairs with help
23 months	Hops in place
25 months	Walks on toes

What Influences Early Childhood Development

As you can see, the first two years of a child's life are very dynamic. A newborn infant is basically helpless, but by the time a child is two years old, many steps have already been made toward independent action and life-long abilities. Whether or not development will occur in a maximal and timely manner depends on a combination of crucial factors. Heredity is the initial factor influencing development. Children with short parents, for example, will generally be shorter than children whose parents are tall. Weight is also partially determined by heredity. Heredity, however, only partially controls a child's potential for development. Equally influential are factors appearing after birth, particularly nutrition, affection, and stimulation.

Nutrition for infants and toddlers is crucial and irreplaceable. During these years is when a great deal of growth, both of the body and the brain, takes place. Failure to give a young child proper nutrition can cause permanent losses in terms of physical and mental development. Proper nutrition begins at birth. Breast milk is nature's way of providing infants with an appropriate balance of fat, protein, nutrients, and antibodies. If breast-feeding is not desired or unfeasible, formulas can provide a good substitute. As your baby grows, a balanced diet is essential.

Giving children a balanced diet of vegetables, fruits, grains, protein, and dairy products assures they will avoid malnutrition. Malnutrition is a serious problem for many children world-wide. Severe malnutrition can lead to a disease called marasmus where the child's body is wasted and which can eventually end in death. A second disease, which appears in the presence of an diet lacking enough protein, is known as kwashiorkor. The symptoms of kwashiorkor include a swollen belly, listlessness, irritability, hair loss, and body rashes. Malnutrition also causes stunted growth and lowered mental capacities. Studies have found that the physical problems associated with malnutrition in early life can be remedied, but the brain does not recover.

Affection and stimulation are similarly crucial in a child's physical development. Infants who do not receive attention, love, and interaction quickly acquire symptoms similar to those associated with malnutrition in spite of adequate nutrition. This problem, known as inorganic failure to thrive, can be corrected if intercepted at an early age. If uncorrected, failure to give a child affection and stimulation can result in physical, intellectual, emotional, and social deficiencies.

Physical development is the first signal parents have that their infants are growing into healthy children. Unless there are problems already dictated by heredity, chances are children are developing well if they are given the nutrition and affection they need. Also, young children are fairly resilient. Although they may never recover fully from neglect or malnutrition, they can make great strides in achieving normal development. This two-year period of time consists of rapid change and important developmental strides. Your fascination with your child's growth can be complete as you better understand the physical milestones from birth to two. ❀

Physical Milestones: Childhood

Following the rapid physical development of infancy and the toddler stage, children's growth slows and becomes more consistent. From the age of three until puberty, significant changes happen, but at a much slower rate than occurred during the first two years of life. Throughout childhood, the skills and physical abilities begun during infancy and toddlerhood continue to develop in complexity and refinement. This development includes obvious physical changes, continued brain growth, and enhancement of motor skills. While development is not as sensitive to debilitating factors as in younger years, children still require protection from various elements to develop into healthy and skillful adolescents.

Recall the concepts of physical development listed in the previous chapter. They include the following:

1. Physical development is tied to every other form of child development.

2. Physical development can be used as a barometer to measure successful development in other areas.

3. Physical abilities are used for different purposes at different stages.

4. As children get older, they first use their physical abilities as a means of social participation.

5. Progressing through the stages of development, children begin to use their physical development as a means of social status.

6. As puberty approaches, physical development translates into body image, which can have significant consequences in the lives of adolescents.

While all these concepts are important, the most applicable to this stage of child development are

298 ❀ Understand Child Development

numbers four and five. You will first notice your children begin to use their newfound skills to play with other children. The first interactions may seem clumsy and awkward, but young children gradually learn how to participate socially. As they grow, children eventually depend on their bodies to give them identity and social status. Social values make this especially important in the lives of young boys. Boys are encouraged to develop skills associated with athletics. As a result, many motor skills are more refined in boys than in girls. However, social status is determined by physical development for both girls and boys. You may recall from your elementary school years which children were "popular" while others were excluded from many activities depending on their ability to perform physical tasks.

Physical Growth

Children between the ages of about three and eleven carry on a fairly consistent rate of growth, although "growth spurts" are common. The average child will gain about five pounds and grow two to three inches each year. In early childhood, parents may begin to notice individual differences in their children's growth rate and body size, which become increasingly evident throughout these years. Bones become longer and stronger. "Baby fat" is replaced by muscle, and children begin to take on more adult proportions. Between the ages of six and seven, children have usually lost and regrown their first tooth, and by the end of childhood, most children have replaced all their baby teeth with permanent ones.

Girls generally develop faster during childhood than boys do. By age nine, most girls have surpassed boys in height, and girls usually reach certain stages first. For example, girls will often lose their first tooth before boys. Boys, on the other hand, develop more muscle than girls, who are accumulating more fat. Other developmental differences can be observed between racial and ethnic groups. Children of certain races, for example, will be shorter than their peers while others will often be taller. Physical growth can greatly impact a child's social status and acceptance by peers during this stage. Perhaps the greatest example of this is the exclusion of obese children from friendship circles. Such problems can severely influence the child's behavior, emotional well-being, and social skills.

Brain Development

Throughout childhood, the brain continues to mature, making it possible for children to succeed at more tasks. As your children get older, you may notice increases in attention, language, coordination, logical thinking, perception, imagination, and memory. These are certainly attributed to steady brain development. During early childhood, the left side of the brain grows quite rapidly, corresponding to the great strides made in language and communication, which the left side controls. Children begin to show a preference for their right or left hand, also controlled by hemispheres of the brain. Centers of the brain controlling balance, body movement, and alertness also gradually develop. As children get older, the section of the brain responsible for thought and consciousness grows further, accounting for children's increasing ability to think about problems, apply logic, and exercise imagination.

Motor Development

Refinement of motor skills is a continuous process throughout childhood. Gross motor skills, or skills involving large muscle groups, become more coordinated, balanced, and smooth. Fine motor skills, or those requiring detail and small muscle use, also refine. Improvement in these categories of movement is evident when you watch children take care of their bodies, play, run, and write. The following section gives an overall picture of the capabilities of children at different ages.

Age Developmental Skills

2-3 years old

Walks rhythmically; runs; jumps with both feet; throws ball awkwardly; changes clothes; uses utensils.

3-4 years old

Walks up and down stairs; uses arms when jumping and hopping; catches ball by trapping against chest; fastens large buttons; uses scissors.

4-5 years old

Runs smoothly; gallops; jumps with greater strength; uses body rotation and weight when throwing; catches ball with hands; dresses self unassisted; follows line with scissors; copies letters and shapes.

5-6 years old

Runs faster and walks with greater balance; skips; throws and catches skillfully; rides a bike; uses a knife to cut food; ties shoes; draws people; copies numbers and some words.

After age six, children continue to refine the skills they have already begun. Their bodies get stronger, so they can run faster, jump higher and farther, and throw faster and farther. They become more accurate and coordinated. They learn how to involve their entire body in movements. Writing becomes more legible and pictures more detailed and accurate. Boys and girls develop obvious differences in both gross and fine motor skills. Boys are generally better at activities involving gross motor skills while girls usually have better fine motor skills. These differences are more likely attributed to children's environment and social influences than to genetic advantages.

What Influences Childhood Development

As in any stage of growth and development, there are certain factors which will either maximize growth or create problems for the developing person. These influences can often be controlled by parents, and a basic understanding of them will help you do the best for your children as they approach adolescence.

Heredity is obviously a key factor in the development of children. A child's genetic code dictates how much a child should grow and tells the body how much of specific growth hormones should be released. However, heredity only writes a portion of your child's future for healthy growth and development. Other things which can have significant influence include emotional support, nutrition, illness, and injury.

Infants and toddlers respond to emotional support, affection, and love with physical growth and health. Infants who fail to receive stimulation early in life do not develop the same as other babies. The same is true for older children. Exposure to constant stress and emotional deprivation has several effects on children's development. They will have more respiratory and intestinal illnesses than other children. In some cases they do not grow at the same rate as other children, developing deprivation dwarfism. If a child's emotional environment is improved early, growth will resume at a normal rate, but if unrecognized, these children are permanently injured.

Nutrition plays a crucial role in children's physical development. You may notice your child's appetite lessens during this stage, which is understandable since children's growth slows after toddlerhood. However, children still need a balanced diet of fruits, vegetables, grains, dairy products, and proteins. Fatty and sugary foods should be minimized to assure greater health in the future. This time is often indicative of future health problems such as obesity, and establishing good eating habits now can reduce such risks. Malnutrition is also a threat for many children. Inadequate nutrition can reduce a child's physical, intellectual, and motor skills development.

Most children are fairly healthy during childhood. Children may suffer from problems with their eyes, ears, and teeth which can often be corrected with medical intervention. Other health problems can be more serious and can inhibit normal development. Asthma, for example, is the greatest cause of absence from school and of childhood hospitalization. Serious and chronic illnesses can produce in children academic, social, and emotional problems, but these problems can be reversed with careful intervention.

Injury is a constant threat to growing children who are excited about life and exploring the use of their developing bodies in every way possible. In fact, accidental injuries are the leading cause of death among children. Prevention of accidents requires careful monitoring, changing of a child's environment, and safety education appropriate for children of varying ages.

Children are amazing, resilient beings, but they are not indestructible. They need attentive care as they work their way through childhood and approach adolescence. Their bodies, which are not as fragile as they

304 ❀ Understand Child Development

once were, still need many things in order to develop to their potential. Successfully providing safety, nutrition, medical care, and emotional stability will help ensure your children grow happily and healthily and reach each childhood milestone in a timely manner. ❀

Puberty

Throughout childhood, physical growth and development have been steady and predictable. Abilities constantly improved as children's bodies became more capable of performing more complex tasks. As your child approaches the teenage years, however, this reliability will be thrown off its course with the onset of puberty, or the period of physical growth changing children into adults. The changes presented during puberty are numerous and fairly sudden. Physical changes are accompanied by emotional, social, and behavioral adjustments. Making puberty especially difficult for many adolescents is the fact that each child develops at an individual rate. It is during this stage of development that the sixth developmental concept becomes very prominent: As puberty approaches, physical development translates into body image, which can have significant consequences in the lives of adolescents.

The noticeable physical changes of puberty are set off by hormones. In girls, the ovaries begin to release estrogen into the bloodstream around the age of nine. In boys, the testes begin to release testosterone around age ten. These hormones signal the body to begin making changes in physical growth and to start the maturation of sexual characteristics.

Physical Growth

The increased presence of estrogen and testosterone first influences physical growth. Children suddenly experience a growth spurt where they rapidly gain weight and height. On average, teenagers gain about forty pounds and grow ten inches during the years of puberty. Girls usually finish growing by age sixteen, while boys continue growing until about age seventeen-and-a-half. The pattern of growth during puberty begins with the legs, feet, and hands, and then the torso follows.

Boys and girls proportions begin to adjust so they more resemble adults. Boys grow taller, their shoulders broaden, their legs get longer, and they get more muscular. Girls gain more width in their hips and accumulate more fat in their arms, legs, and waist.

Internal organs also grow and develop during adolescence. The heart, lungs, eyes, and tonsils all change during this period. Oil, sweat, and odor glands become more active at the onset of puberty. These changes all have their impact on the growing person. Greater lung capacity and better circulation, for example, improve physical endurance and athletic abilities. Becoming oilier and sweatier, on the other hand, can cause problems like acne, which is a very sensitive issue for teens.

The sudden changes in a child's body brought about by puberty are very significant, both emotionally and socially, for children. For example, girls who enter puberty earlier than their peers generally feel awkward, self-conscious, and they experience social difficulties. Boys who develop earlier than their peers, on the other hand, are often admired, self-confident, and considered attractive. The emotional and social impact of puberty can have very detrimental effects. Many young women, for example, become overly concerned to the point of obsession with their widening hips and increased fat. Changing their body composition through dieting and eating disorders becomes the focus of attention because their bodies don't fit a prescribed mold of thinness. These problems are very serious, both mentally and physically, and are potentially life-threatening.

Sexual Maturation

In addition to the rapid physical growth taking place during puberty, it is also a time when sex characteristics develop and mature. The maturation of sex characteristics involves both primary and secondary characteristics. Primary sex characteristics include the organs involved in reproduction. For girls this includes the uterus, ovaries, and vagina. In boys this includes the penis, scrotum, and testes. Secondary sex characteristics are those visible on the outside of the body. For example, girls develop breasts and grow wider in the hips. Boys grow taller, get wider shoulders, and their voices get significantly lower. Both sexes begin to grow underarm and pubic hair. Girls and boys develop these characteristics at different ages and at different rates. There is also wide individual variance.

Sexual Maturation in Girls

The appearance of noticeable sex characteristics occurs about a year after estrogen has begun its work. Breast "buds" begin to appear, on average, at about the age of ten, and pubic hair growth shows up a year later. A girl's first menstrual period, or menarche, is often used as a measure that puberty has arrived, although it occurs late in the maturation process between the ages of twelve and thirteen. The following year completes breast development and pubic hair growth. It also takes about a year for a girl to be capable of becoming pregnant in spite of the fact she is menstruating. On average, a girl has completed the sequence of maturation by the time she is sixteen years old.

Sexual Maturation in Boys

About a year following the appearance of testosterone in the blood stream, or around age eleven, boys begin to experience noticeable changes. First, their testes and scrotum grow larger. Soon after, pubic hair appears, followed by growth of the penis. Boys experience their first ejaculation of seminal fluid, known as spermarche, between the ages of thirteen and fifteen. It usually takes about a year before mature or live sperm are produced. Around this time a boy's voice lowers and he soon notices coarse hair on his face. This sequence of development and maturation is usually finished around the age of eighteen.

Factors Influencing Development during Puberty

We have already described how being female or male influences the onset of puberty and the rate at which development occurs. There are many other things which have as much or more importance while children are changing into adults. Heredity is one aspect which helps determine when children will begin puberty. Sisters, for example, are very likely to start menstruating at near the same age. Studies of twins show similar trends.

Body composition plays an important role in development. Boys and girls who have a higher percentage of body fat tend to start puberty at earlier ages than their thin peers. This is especially true for girls, influencing the age at which they begin to menstruate. Girls who are very physically active and who participate in activities such as dancing or running begin their menstrual cycle later than average. Other girls who are inactive and have more body fat often start their menstrual cycle a year or so earlier than average.

Overall health and nutrition are very important for normal and timely development. Adolescence is a period of rapid and crucial growth. In order to facilitate this development, teenagers need to make sure they are eating properly and getting all the necessary nutrients. Nutrition can affect the onset of puberty. For example, one hundred years ago both girls and boys began puberty about five to six years later than they do today. This is attributed to the fact that proper nutrition and adequate health care allow our bodies to develop when they are ready. Health and nutrition are important for other reasons as well. Many teenagers do not eat enough of several nutrients, including iron, calcium, riboflavin, and magnesium. This deficiency can create immediate problems such as tiredness and irritability or may affect the growing person in the long term. Also, establishing a healthy diet at this age is important for ensuring good life-long habits.

Of serious concern is the fact that many teenagers begin engaging in very harmful activities during this stage that threaten their well-being and even their lives. A common threat to girls, as a result of their inability to conform to standards of beauty, is participation in eating disorders. In addition, social changes which accompany puberty bring new pressures and temptations. Use of drugs and alcohol, for example, is prevalent by the time adolescents graduate from high school. Regular participation in using these substances increases a teenager's risk of addiction and abuse, permanent injury to body and mind, and even death. Other predictable changes in the experience of adolescents are the new feelings of sexual excitement and curiosity about the opposite sex. Acting upon these feelings and becoming sexually active can have serious consequences for young teenagers. Studies have shown that most of these teenagers ignore precautions of the risks of getting pregnant or acquiring a variety of sexually transmitted diseases, including AIDS.

In spite of the indestructible attitude many teenagers have, the great changes associated with puberty and the transition from childhood to adulthood make puberty a very sensitive time. Teenagers' bodies are growing very rapidly and need care to ensure proper and healthy development. Teens need to eat well, receive enough of the necessary vitamins, and avoid damaging their bodies by engaging in eating disorders, substance abuse, and premature sexual activity. These things, in addition to enjoying a supportive emotional environment, will greatly help adolescents grow into healthy and well-adjusted adults. ❀

Prosocial Behavior

Most adults can look at others around them and distinguish between those whose social skills are well-developed and those who lack these skills. A fundamental aspect of positive social skills is the ability to participate in prosocial behavior. Prosocial behavior may be defined as actions which benefit another person, done without expectation of a reward in return. These actions are highly connected to morality, or acting in ways which help rather than harm others and demonstrating concern for another's welfare. Individuals who take on a prosocial orientation take into consideration the whole of an individual's physical, emotional, mental, and spiritual well-being. Specific demonstrations of prosocial behavior include helpful, kind, giving, caring, cooperative, and generous actions.

Prosocial behavior develops gradually as a child's social interactions mature. Evidence of prosocial behavior in infants appears when they interact with their parents. For example, a one year old giving a parent a toy is a demonstration of developing positive social skills. When toddlers begin helping around the house by picking up their toys, they are showing their growing ability to interact prosocially. They learn to help others in distress, to provide comfort, and to show empathy. The older children get, the more they recognize the value of prosocial behavior, and they begin to willingly help others.

The development of prosocial behavior depends on a series of developmental events. First, a child must have the ability to pay attention to other people's needs rather than just his or her own. Children require the ability to accurately interpret social situations and look at things from other people's perspectives. Following this, children must decide whether or not to help another person. If the decision is made to help, a child must demonstrate self-control to act upon the choice.

Research conducted by Nancy Eisenberg (1992) determined several stages of prosocial development. The following section outlines these stages from preschool age to adulthood.

Stages of Prosocial Development

Hedonistic

Age: Most preschoolers and many elementary-school children
Description: Hedonists seek to fulfill their own pleasure. These children focus on what they will gain or lose by helping or whether they like another person well enough to help.

Needs-oriented

Age: Some preschoolers and many older children
Description: Children with this orientation have concern for others but don't directly show sympathy and don't discuss feelings such as guilt.

Interpersonal or Stereotyped Approval

Age: Some elementary and high school students
Description: These children emphasize what a "good" person would do or what will bring social approval.

Self-Reflecting Empathy

Age: Many high school students
Description: These individuals express sympathy, understand others' perspectives, and verbally recognize how their action or inaction would lead to various feelings (i.e., happiness or guilt).

Transitional

Age: Some high school students and adults
Description: These people emphasize, but do not clearly express, personal values, social conditions, and the need to protect individual rights.

Strongly Internalized

Age: Few high-school students and adults
Description: These people focus on internalized values and responsibilities. They desire to improve society, believe in the dignity of all people, and wish to maintain self-respect by living one's values.

Cultivating Prosocial Behavior

While infants enter this world with primitive forms of prosocial and empathetic behavior, it takes years for their initial helpfulness and cooperation to develop into internal values about kindness and moral actions. The development of prosocial behavior corresponds with increased skill during social interactions, greater understanding about the world, and more knowledge about emotions. However, some children have a more difficult time exhibiting prosocial behavior. In homes where parents are inattentive to the feelings of others and adopt a selfish attitude when faced with choices regarding whether or not they should help another, their children grow to entertain similar attitudes. Parents have the same potential to raise children who are sympathetic, willingly helpful, and cooperative when faced with the needs of others. The difference lies in what parents continually do while their children are growing and learning how to interact with those around them.

The first thing parents need to do to cultivate prosocial behavior in their children is to be a positive example of helpfulness. When your children witness your concern for others and your willingness to do that which will benefit the people around you, your children will follow that example. An important part of this principle is that prosocial behavior is not appropriate only among peers and those outside the family. Children need to observe your helpfulness and kindness to members of your family. Most likely they will rarely see you participating in acts of kindness outside of your home. Ultimately, to help children develop prosocial behavior, parents need to do it first.

A second key to children's development of prosocial behavior is to help them participate in caring acts. Discuss with your children various situations when it is appropriate to help others and to be kind. Provide opportunities which demand cooperation, kindness, and sympathy. A family, for example, might take advantage of the chance to serve another less fortunate family at Christmas and act as a "Secret Santa." Getting the whole family involved in this type of activity allows children to actively participate in helping others. This means that parents should not be the sole contributors. Children should be allowed to give what they can, such as money or toys. Families could also visit a nearby hospital or rest home to provide companionship for the people who are there. Seeing first-hand the needs of others and experiencing the act of caring propels the development of prosocial action.

Talking about feelings is a final way to help children cultivate prosocial behavior. The benefit of communicating about emotions is mainly that children learn to identify feelings of their own and recognize feelings in others. As they more fully understand how to identify emotions, children become more competent in sympathizing with others, respecting others' perspectives, and noticing when others are in need of help and care.

Parents all wish for their children to enjoy success in their social interactions. One of the primary elements of positive social skills is the ability to engage in prosocial behaviors. Children need to understand the value of helping, caring, giving, and sympathizing with those around them. The greater their skill and development of these behaviors, the more success they will enjoy in their relationships and in life. 🏵

Memory

Memory, the mental ability to retain and recall impressions and past experiences, has an interesting and fascinating story. Recent neural research permits us to understand, for instance, that we have natural built-in memory distributed throughout the brain. This is connected to the five senses, giving each person visual, auditory, kinesthetic (touch), olfaction (smell), and taste memories. These appear to work at birth and improve with maturity. In addition, these natural memories provide some other interesting features.

People inherit different levels of ability in each of the natural memories so that one person may have better visual or auditory memory than another. These inherited abilities tend to influence how much success we achieve in different types of activities. If, for instance, you have good visual memory, you will probably be more successful in those activities which require extensive use of this memory—public school is one of these.

Our abilities are not simply a matter of what we inherit. Our abilities are influenced by what we learn. Researchers have found that memory improves based on the need for it and application. In countries where older people tell children about social and family traditions, the children develop an enhanced ability in auditory memory. This occurs because they use it more often as they participate in their life experiences. This and other discoveries have stimulated the search for new ways to improve memory.

The development of memory begins at birth. Many people believe that infants retain basically none of their experiences. Research has found that this is not necessarily true. Young infants do lose many memories very quickly. As they get older, their ability to retain information and experiences gradually improves. However, memory can be maximized in young infants depending upon the learning situation, the infant's motivation to remember, and the relevance of the situation to the infant's experience. It is also apparent that increased memory corresponds with brain maturation and language development during the first two years of life. Later, during childhood, memory is very well-developed. A child's inability to perform as well as adults in different areas of knowledge is probably more related to their inexperience than to deficiencies in memory.

The Importance of Memory

Most people have known someone who has a problem such as Alzheimer's disease and whose memory skills are seriously debilitated. How well can' they function in their homes or communities without the ability to remember? Imagine how humans would perform without memories. We would basically be incapable of performing daily tasks, building relationships, or any other typical activity. This is the most obvious reason memory is important, but many other reasons exist.

Memory is highly valuable as children go through the education system. However, a good memory does not just improve grades. A good memory increases listening abilities and retention of interesting facts while increasing the effectiveness of time spent learning. People with effective memories tend to age more slowly, and can be more aware of others because they do not forget important relationship events.

Memory is associated with important cultural values. For example, our concept of the world today suggests that those with greater knowledge live more interesting lives; at least that is the basis for the "earn what you learn" theory. Embedded in the theory of democratic education is the idea that knowledge is fundamental to successful participation in society. However, when people of all ages work on increasing their memories, they are doing more than improving their potential for academic success. There is considerable evidence that school success is only one life situation, though an important one. Various forms of memory are useful in situations other than school, which greatly contribute to success in life and make lives more significant.

Another valuable aspect of memory development revolves around the fact that we live in a time when there is much more information available to us than at any other time in human history. Its availability has created the need for us to think about how to use this information more effectively. We must accelerate our abilities to acquire, organize, and use new information.

This abundance of information has created major changes in virtually every aspect of our lives. The most obvious examples include communication, business, industry, and international relations. In all of these, the ability to send, receive, and analyze information has determined success or failure. Those who understand how to accelerate information processing are those who have survived and succeeded.

Factors Influencing Memory Development

Memory takes time to develop. Newborns' abilities to remember things are extremely fragile, and development of memory progresses gradually.

Research indicates that memory increases in infants at a comparable rate to brain maturation.

Understanding this, we may conjecture that factors influencing brain development will likewise impact the development of a capable memory. Things such as proper nutrition, emotional support and affection, and freedom from injury or illness probably all have a place in ensuring a well-developed memory.

Of greater significance than environmental factors such as healthiness is the ability to apply certain memory strategies. Unless there is something neurologically wrong, individuals should not be classified as having "good" or "bad" memories. Instead, it is evident that people who we usually consider skillful in recalling information are actually those who have learned to apply specific memory strategies. While it is true that some people enjoy some skills naturally, making them initially more successful, anyone can develop memory strategies. For this reason, there should be no need for certain people to feel like they have failed or are unsuccessful. The following paragraphs will briefly describe seven principles of memory and their importance in developing memory skills.

Meaning

The human brain is organized to store information that is meaningful. Information that is not meaningful is much more difficult to organize and store. For example, you will quickly forget a list of nonsense words like rif, fod, kip, and dur. To help you out, there are at least three ways to make something have meaning: (1) familiarity; (2) patterns; and (3) rhymes.

Organization

The brain is highly organized. That is why more information is retained and recall is better if you organize the information you are trying to memorize. You will be using methods of categorization. Not only is it easy, it is fun; and it makes learning more interesting.

Attention

It is difficult to remember anything to which you do not pay attention. Selective attention is the ability to screen out distractions in order to concentrate or focus on something you wish to remember. Attention improves naturally as you mature, and therefore, it can be improved with practice.

Association

You will better remember things that seem to be associated with another. Some believe that associating individual items makes them more meaningful, and that is why association improves memory. Whatever the reason, associating or linking ideas together improves memory.

Visualization

Whether you know it or not, you have a wonderful ability to create an internal stimulus by yourself;

this is called visualization. It is like imagining, fantasizing, or daydreaming. You do quite a bit of this because it is pleasurable, but you can also use this ability to improve memory. There are three ways to use visualization. These are: (1) vividness; (2) substitution; and (3) exaggeration.

Chunking

Chunking is a special form of memory organization. Because it is so useful, you should learn more about it. Chunking entails grouping or categorizing information so that you can remember the chunks plus everything inside. Suppose you learn about birds and place fourteen different kinds of birds in this "chunk." Remembering "birds" will help you remember all fourteen types. As another example, the seven memory principles could be separated and each one called a "chunk."

Mnemonics

Mnemonics is a specialized form of association. Usually, it is an association which increases the pleasure of remembering for the person who is trying to do it. Four types of mnemonics are: (1) stories; (2) links; (3) first letters; and (4) locations.

As you can see, we as individuals play a very important role in the development of memory. It is not something left entirely to nature and inherited abilities. By learning specific strategies, and then repeatedly practicing, applying, and discussing them, we can facilitate our memory's development. As we teach these strategies to our children, we give them a skill which will help them be more successful in every aspect of their lives.   ✿

(This chapter is adapted from *Getting and Keeping a Good Memory*, by A. Lynn Scoresby, Ph.D.)

Empathy

If you accept the perspective that moral behavior is doing what helps others and avoiding what hurts others, then you will understand that empathy is a major characteristic required for moral actions. Empathy is the ability to sense vicariously the emotions and needs of other people, to react sympathetically, and to help them. Empathetic people use this sense to act with compassion, a sense of caring, and sensitive attention. Empathy produces guilt, which can help prevent hurtful acts against both oneself and others. Research informs us that children display a kind of empathy from birth. If they have adequate examples, discussion of their feelings, and praise, children expand their empathy for others as they mature.

The opposite of empathy is defensiveness. Defensive people shift responsibility for their actions to someone else. This allows them to justify immorality by avoiding guilt. They hide their feelings and thoughts, excessively fear the disapproval of others, avoid new or strange situations, act with aggression, alienate themselves, and are insensitive to the feelings of others. Defensiveness contributes to immoral, irresponsible behavior.

While certain elements of empathy may be displayed at birth, its presence is displayed more readily when children become more aware of themselves, or upon the emergence of a sense of self. You may notice how toddlers begin to respond to another child's sadness or fear by giving the other child things which provide themselves with comfort. Simple actions such as hugs or kind comments may be a part of this empathetic reaction, or the toddler might give the other child objects of worth such as a favorite doll or blanket. Later, with increased language development, empathy is demonstrated more in statements that reflect understanding.

The Value of Empathy in Society

Successful interactions and relationships with others depend upon our ability to look at things from others' perspectives and to feel what others feel. In other words, positive relationships and interactions depend upon empathy. This is particularly evident in the observation of children whose social skills are lacking. Aggressive and angry children have a hard time imagining others' thoughts and feelings. Without having an awareness of another person's point of view, they fail to feel guilt for their actions and are unable to recognize how another feels when mistreated and abused. Because of this lack of perspective, they easily hurt other people and have a difficult time making and keeping friends.

Individuals with a well-developed sense of empathy are contributors to society. They are skilled in making decisions which will benefit as many people as possible. They are aware of how their actions, behaviors, and attitudes influence people around them. Consider the following two anecdotes and the empathy encouraged by the children's parents.

The Hendersons were concerned about comments their son, Rob, made about a boy at school. One day after Rob spoke harshly and critically about this boy, Mr. Henderson asked Rob about him. "Well," Rob began, "the other day in class, I was talking and he made fun of what I said. Then, a group of us were standing in the lunch line and he jumped in front of me, saying he was late for class. He is so stupid!" Mr. Henderson asked, "Do you know why he acted that way?" He knew that the other boy's parents were divorcing and asked Rob if he knew. "No," Rob replied. "How do you think children might feel when their parents get a divorce?" the father asked. "I wonder if that would make him feel strange enough to do what he did." Mr. Henderson could see Rob's feelings soften somewhat, and he asked, "Do you think there is any way to help him?" They continued talking until Rob recognized that the other boy might benefit from some friendly attention.

Susan was ten years old and planning a birthday party. She wanted to invite her friends. A new girl had recently moved into the neighborhood. Susan and her friends did not yet know her very well, and Susan's shyness made her resent the new girl somewhat. When Susan asked her best friend about inviting the new girl to the party, her friend said, "Don't invite her. Just have our friends come." When Susan and her mother were preparing the invitations, her mother suggested that Susan invite the new girl. "I don't want her to come," Susan replied. "Why not?" her mother asked. Feeling accused, Susan retorted, "Shelley doesn't want her to come either." "Hmm," her mother said, "do you remember how lonely you felt when we first moved here and how happy you were when Heather and Tami brought over welcome gifts?" "Yeah," Susan said. "Well," said her mother, "don't you think we should help this new girl feel welcome too?"

Factors Influencing the Development of Empathy

The development of empathy is a fragile process. Although infants are born with the capacity for empathy and demonstrate forms of empathy very early in their lives, we can't assume everyone will grow through childhood into adolescence and adulthood as empathetic individuals. A child's experiences greatly determine whether or not empathy will properly develop. One of the most important indicators of successful development of empathy is parents' treatment of their children. Parents who are quick to encourage their children and who treat them with respect, warmth, sensitivity, and concern raise children who show concern toward others. These children react toward their peers with empathy, recognizing another child's distress and making steps to remedy the problem.

The situation is much different among children whose parents frequently punish, scold, degrade, and abuse them. These behaviors toward children severely impair the development of empathy. These children do not know how to react toward others who are suffering, and they often respond to problems with fear, anger, and aggression. These are all characteristics of defensiveness, the opposite characteristic of empathy.

After consistent exposure to a destructive environment, the development of empathy is not lost on children. Intervention is possible when children are taught about emotions. Asked to identify and discuss their own feelings, as well as how other people might feel, children eventually learn to adopt others' perspectives and consider how others feel in various situations. Learning to recognize what children personally feel allows them to discover empathy and to sympathize with the experiences of others. This helps them limit and eventually discontinue their own immoral behavior and overcome their fearful or angry attitudes.

Ability to talk about and understand the feelings of oneself and of others is dependent on knowledge about emotions. A young child might feel a certain way but be unable to describe those feelings with words such as happy, excited, frustrated, worried, calm, or lonely. The more familiar a child becomes with emotions and the vocabulary used to describe them, the more a child can exercise empathy. For this reason, it is invaluable for parents to communicate often with their children about emotions in a variety of situations. The earlier communication begins, the more highly competent children will be in empathizing with the people around them.

Empathy is a crucial interpersonal skill. Knowledge about emotions allows children to sympathize with the situations of others and recognize others' needs. Perhaps the most important aspect of empathy is its influence on a person's actions. The ability to see things from another person's perspective and take that perspective into consideration when preparing to act enables children, adolescents, and adults to behave morally.   ❈

(Portions of this chapter excerpted from *Bringing Up Moral Children in an Immoral World*, by A. Lynn Scoresby, Ph.D.)

Social Competence

As children are socialized into society they learn the skills necessary to successfully interact with other people. Through the example of their parents and their exposure to various social situations including school, church, and peer play groups children learn what is required to make friends, adapt to different people, express themselves well, and act in social circles. Social competence, or the ability to effectively participate with others, is demonstrated even in infancy. Although it is commonly believed that infants are entirely passive, existing only to be molded into what society wishes, infants actually initiate social interactions and actively maintain their parents' responses. Their limited demonstrations of social competence begin simply as they fixate on the human face and respond to human voices immediately after birth.

The development of social competence is a continual process. Parents can observe their children gaining competence in social situations when children learn to share, to express empathy, to communicate about their needs and wants, and to think less egotistically. However, even a toddler's apparently selfish statements and actions are the beginnings of an understanding about self and others. This step of development produces the groundwork for further social skills.

Characteristics of Socially Competent Children

Competence in any given area means that a person has skill, knowledge, or experience to perform well. Different areas of competence may be measured in several ways. You might think of academic competence, for example, which is often measured by tests and grades. Other forms of competence include creative skills and emotional stability. Social competence can generally be divided into three categories: interactions with adults, interactions with peers, and expressions of self.

Young children who demonstrate competency in their interactions with adults are skilled in several ways. These children understand how to get the attention of parents and other adults in socially-acceptable ways. Socially-competent children also recognize adults as sources of help. These children can alternate between expressions of hostility and displays of affection toward adults.

Children in this stage of development are also learning to interact with their peers. Young children who are socially competent have begun to both lead and follow other children. They can compete and will demonstrate feelings of both hostility and affection to the children they come in contact with.

Young children begin to develop a sense of self. When they are socially competent, they learn to express themselves in some important ways. First of all, they praise their own accomplishments and show pride in their achievements. Also, these children become involved in role-playing adult behavior. Apparently, they look forward to growing up and engaging in adult activities.

Social competence is tied to additional things. It is difficult, for example, for a child with low levels of language skills to interact and communicate with peers and adults. Inability to communicate well might also cause a child to inappropriately act out in situations which require communication but where the child feels incapable and distressed. While good social skills alone can encourage children's overall success, a combination of several skills such as academic, emotional, physical, and social abilities all work together to help a child succeed.

Promoting Social Competence

While infants enter the world with a natural ability to interact with others, social competence is also a learned trait. Children progressively gain the social skills necessary to interact successfully, to adapt to various situations and people, and to contribute to society. For example, you will notice toddlers are very focused on their personal needs and wants. As they get older, they begin to pay better attention to the needs of others. Another example of improving skills is a child's entry strategies. Young children will often act in negative ways to get attention or will enter a conversation in an inappropriate or distracting way. In time, children develop more socially-acceptable entry strategies. For example, they learn how to get attention by asking for help. When entering a conversation, they will make relevant comments which don't direct negative attention toward themselves, or they will wait to be addressed. These skills become very necessary as children try to make friends, work to be successful in school, and prepare to become positive members of society.

Parents and other care givers play a very important role in their children's development of social competence. Parenting style particularly can provide an indication of whether or not children will learn positive social strategies. When parents show several characteristics, they foster competence in their children. These parents enjoy their young children, talk to them so the children can understand, and focus on their children's learning and happiness. The parents place minimal emphasis on neatness of the house, for example, because they are more concerned that their children have a fun and safe learning environment. They encourage their children's learning through exploration and risk-taking, while simultaneously setting limits appropriate to the child's age. The parents themselves usually maintain a positive attitude and a busy schedule.

Other parenting styles do not encourage the same social competence in children. Depressed and disorganized parents, for example, cannot provide a stimulating learning environment for their children. Constant supervision and overprotectiveness also diminish children's ability to explore, satisfy curiosity, and assert independence. Children of parents who are inattentive, abusive, and neglectful also have a difficult time developing social competence as they get older.

Other factors in addition to the parents' characteristics contribute to children's success in developing social competence. A child's personality and temperament can be very difficult for parents to manage creatively. For example, parents might become frustrated when they repeatedly have to instruct or reprimand. It becomes easier to use simple commands like, "Don't" or "Stop," than to explain the reasons why certain behavior is inappropriate or to provide alternative entertainment. Also, a family's context may provide special difficulties. Oldest children often have greater social competence than second children. Parents tend to have more energy, patience, and creativity with their first children than with subsequent children. Other factors such as a child's varying abilities, parental support, school organization, and peer acceptance also contribute to a child's development. Children who feel they can succeed in several areas, receive positive feedback from their parents, are exposed to several subjects in school, and are allowed to participate with their friends don't feel the need to act in socially-unacceptable ways to be noticed and acknowledged. They don't need to cover up their inadequacies or lack of self-confidence by acting out. Instead, they enjoy circumstances which allow them to work at developing their social competence and become more skilled in social situations.

Social competence is a valuable aspect of development. Children need families and environments which stimulate their social skills. As they become more able to succeed in social situations, communicate with many different types of people, and develop friendships they learn the skills which will serve them their entire lives. Social competence is crucial in every situation people find themselves in, and early development sets the stage for success in those times and places.   ❀

Independent Work Habits

Work is often considered a necessary evil. It can be seen by parents as a major source of stress and contention. However, most of our needs and wants cannot be fulfilled without consistent work. Families require work in the home to be shared between family members in order to ensure survival and success. It is also within the family where children first learn attitudes toward work and develop work-related behaviors. Children's experiences with work within the home influence their experiences at school and eventually their performance in jobs and careers. When parents encourage and expect their children to work, children learn concepts of responsibility and dependability. The development of these concepts requires that children be taught to work independently, or to be able to start and finish work without excessive supervision.

Our children come to us depending entirely on us for their well-being and care. In the middle years of childhood and thereafter, our children can be cured of dependency and the effects of our indulgence if they are able to develop compassion, a willingness to be of service to others, and responsibility for self. When we give chores to children and carefully help them to complete them, they learn that doing work—and doing it well— is a matter of personal responsibility. Everyone benefits from the sense of mastery that results from accomplishment. When children achieve, they feel stronger and more in control of themselves and their lives.

The ability to work independently follows certain developmental stages. These stages are labeled and described below.

1. Pretend work

Work begins for children as play. You may observe young children enjoying picking up their rooms because it is like a game.

2. Imitation

Children begin to copy what they see adults do. They will "play house," for example, and imitate the roles their parents fill in work situations.

3. Cooperative work
Working together helps children learn how to appropriately begin and complete tasks. It is also how skills develop. Young children are very excited about helping other people work.

4. Individual effort and completion for rewards
Children no longer need to work with others to complete a task, but they often need some type of tangible motivation. For example, a reward of going outside to play will encourage them to get their chores done.

5. Effort and completion for social acceptance
Children begin to notice social expectation for their effort and completion of tasks. In school, for example, they receive recognition from their teachers and peers when they perform well.

6. Internalized work behavior
Eventually, children develop the ability to work independently and complete tasks because of intrinsic satisfaction. They no longer require rewards or external recognition for achievement.

Independent Work Habits Translate into Lifelong Success

The first place where children's abilities to work independently are tested is at school. Children who do well in school have been provided at home with ample opportunity to work independent of adult supervision. On the other hand, some parents might say, "My children will do anything as long as I work with them." Such a pattern of productivity often teaches children to be dependent on the parents as opposed to working independently. Research clearly shows that a child performs better academically when parents assign a task to a child and then indicate that they will return in a few minutes to see how the child is doing.

Unfortunately, some well-meaning parents assign tasks to their children and then end up performing the tasks for them. This practice actually teaches children to wait for adults, because they know the parents will end up performing the task. The result is that the children only learn to perform when an adult is supervising. It is interesting to note that many children carry the same pattern into the school room. For example, an observant person can watch a classroom teacher give an assignment and then notice that some children will not start. The teacher then will walk to those children's sides, explain what needs to be done, and hover around in order to get the children to perform. In most cases, this style of working is a result of a behavior pattern learned in the home. Now consider what will happen to these same children when they become adults and join the competitive work force. Will they be able to succeed in an environment where they are required to show initiative and work independently? Chances are they will not, having failed to develop a habit of independent work.

The result is much different when parents teach the value of independent work. Consider the story of a father who prepared a small garden plot for his daughter. He spent enough time with her to explain about planting, weeding, watering, and even told of the enjoyment the fresh produce would bring. He showed her how to make the rows and plant seeds, and then he left her to do the rest of the work. He showed interest by asking whether or not the plants had come up.

As the plants grew, he showed her about weeding and left her alone to finish. He evaluated her work with her and showed her how to improve. More than this, he took her to other people's gardens and pointed out the difference between the gardens of someone who took care and someone who was indifferent. They talked about the two kinds of gardens, and he explained to her that he wanted her to grow a garden that would be like the gardens of the people who took care. He did not tell her how much weeding or watering she had to do to achieve that goal. He left that for her to discover. He occasionally went with her to check her garden but did not do much to help her unless she asked him to. He talked about what she was doing, though, and pointed to both the good and the less-than-good, hoping to avoid discouraging her.

This girl's first garden wasn't especially good, but the following year she showed interest in trying again. She worked harder, continually encouraged and complimented by her father, and her garden improved. Each successive year she learned new skills and enjoyed greater success. She had learned the values of independent work, responsibility, dependability, and thoroughness, and had developed these positive habits which would serve her through her entire life.

Teaching Children the Value of Independent Work

As infants become toddlers and gain increased control over their bodies, they often desire greater independence. During this time you can begin to teach independent work habits by encouraging and promoting their efforts to do things for themselves. In many cases, however, teaching children how to work independently becomes a serious battle. Your circumstances may discourage you from trying to accomplish this task. Perhaps you spend a long day at your job and have little energy when you return home to spend organizing work for your family. You may feel the battles to get your children to perform chores are not worth the effort and struggle. You may have a financial situation which allows you to hire someone else to perform many of the standard household responsibilities. Regardless of the situation, you can and must instill the value of independent work in your children. There are many opportunities where you can apply this value. For example, your children might take piano lessons and need to practice on a regular schedule. This is only one situation in which you can promote independent work habits.

One of the primary factors influencing children's development of attitudes toward work and work-related behavior is the example they observe in their parents. The first thing you need to do as you approach this developmental stage is to examine your personal reactions and feelings toward work. If, for example, you procrastinate starting projects or jobs, your children will pick up on and copy your behavior. The same is true if you leave several chores or goals unfinished. On the other hand, if you consistently start and complete your activities, your children will most likely follow your lead. Also, how you talk about work sends messages to your children. Grumbling and griping about having to work gives work a negative association, while happily going about your chores teaches children positive attitudes.

Certain types of reinforcement also encourage children to develop independent work habits. Two techniques are particularly effective: "leave and return" and "unexpected reinforcement." "Leave and return" is easy. After starting children on some task, tell them you are leaving and will return in a few moments to see how they are doing. Leave the room, usually for a few seconds at the beginning, and then return. If they are working, praise them and hug them and look at what they are doing. Then repeat the procedure. Gradually lengthen the time between leaving and returning and vary it so that children cannot accurately predict when you will return. Always show interest in their work. If they are not working when you return, simply direct their attention to what needs to be done without criticizing them for dawdling or being lazy, and leave again. Doing this when children are young will help them learn to work by themselves.

"Unexpected reinforcement" is a little different. When children are working, and only then, interrupt them at their work and reward them unexpectedly. One parent, for example, starts her daughter at piano practice. She leaves for a few minutes and then waits until she hears her child playing. Then she returns with some reward, perhaps a small piece of candy, a loving embrace, a compliment. These unexpected rewards encourage children to continue working; if they are not working, they receive no reward. Persistence will come to have pleasant associations for children, and eventually the rewards will be less important.

Eventually, children will have to decide for themselves about the importance of independent work. They will have to discriminate between activities which need to be started and finished and which can be ignored. Some basic questions you can teach your children to ask themselves include: What are the expectations for a task? Are they clearly explained? What promises were made at the time the task was begun? What are the consequences for the children and other people involved if the children finish or stop? By helping children answer these questions, we can teach them to make good choices and to consider how their own actions and ability to work independently impact the people around them. You will have successfully instilled in them some of the most influential values they will every need.   ❀

(Portions of this chapter are excerpted from *Bringing Up Moral Children in an Immoral World,* by A. Lynn Scoresby, Ph.D.)

Bibliography

Becker, W. C. "Consequences of Different Kinds of Parental Discipline." In *Review of Child Development Research*. Vol 1., edited by M. L. Hoffman and L. W. Hoffman, 169-208. New York: Russel Sage, 1964.

Boyce, W. D., and L. C. Jense. *Moral Reasoning: A Psychological-Philosophical Interaction..* Omaha: University of Nebraska Press, 1978.

Decharms, R., and G. H. Moeller. "Values Expressed in American Children's Readers: 1800-1950." *Journal of Abnormal and Social Psychology*. (1962): 64, 136-142.

Eisenberg, N. *The caring child*. Cambridge, MA: Harvard University Press, 1992.

Ekman, P. "Primary Emotions." *Psychology Today* (March 1985):

Gagne, R. M. *The Conditions of Learning* (Third Edition). New York: Holt, Rinehart, and Winston, 1977.

Garvey, C. *Play* (The Developmental Child Series). Cambridge, MA: Harvard University Press, 1977.

Harter, S. "Developmental Differences in the Manifestation of Mastery Motivation on Problem-Solving Tasks." *Child Development*. 1975: 46(2), 370-378.

Helms, D. B., and J. S. Turner. *Lifespan Development* (Second Edition). New York: Holt, Reinhart, and Winston, 1983.

Kellerman, H. "An Epigenetic Theory of Emotions in Early Development." *Emotion: Theory, Research, and Experience,* edited by Plutchik and Kellerman, 1984.

Kohlberg, L. "The Development of Children's Orientations Towards a Moral Order: I. Sequence in the Development of Human Thought." *Vita Human* (1963): 6, 11-33.

LeFrancois, G. R. *Of Children*. Belmont, Calif.: Wadsworth, 1980.

————. *Psychology*. Belmont, Calif.: Wadsworth, 1980.

McClelland, D. C. "Some Social Consequences of Achievement Motivation." In *Nebraska Symposium on Motivation* (Vol. 3), edited by M.R. Jones, Lincoln: University of Nebraska Press, 1955.

Montemayor, R., and M. Eisen. "The Development of Self-Conceptions from Childhood to Adolescence." *Developmental Psychology* (1977): 13, 314-19.

Nelson, K. "Structure and Strategy in Learning to Talk." *Monographs for the Society for Research in Child Development*, 1973, (Serial No. 149) 38 (1-2).

Plutchik, R. *Emotion: A Psychoevolutionary Synthesis*. New York, New York: Harper and Row, 1980.

Schoolar, J. C. *Current Issues in Adolescent Psychiatry*. Chapter One, "Normal Adolescence in Perspective." by Offer, D., and J. Offer. Institute for Psychosomatic and Psychiatric Research and Training, Michael Reese Hospital and Pritzker School of Medicine, University of Chicago, 1984.

Scoresby, A. Lynn, Ph.D. "Empathy." *Bringing Up Moral Children in an Immoral World*. Salt Lake City, Utah: Shadow Mountain Press, 1996.

———. "Independent Work Habits." *Bringing Up Moral Children in an Immoral World*. Salt Lake City, Utah: Shadow Mountain Press, 1998.

———. *Getting and Keeping a Good Memory*. Orem, Utah: Knowledge Gain Publications, 1995.

———. "The Developmental Perspective.." *The Real Power of Parenthood: How To Find and Use it Successfully*. Orem, Utah: Knowledge Gain Publications, 1998.

———. "Windows of Learning." *Windows of Learning: Emotions, Language, Numbers*. Orem, Utah: Knowledge Gain Publications, 1998.

Selman, R. L., and A. P. Selman. "Children's Ideas About Friendship: A New Theory." *Psychology Today* (1979) 13(4), 71-80, 114.

Stevens, S. *The Learning Disabled Child: Ways that Parents Can Help*. John F. Blir Publishers: Winston-Salem, NC, 1980.

Thomas, A., and S. Chess. *Temperament and Development*. New York: Brunner/Mazel, 1977.

Vandell, D. L., K. S. Wilson, and N. R. Buchanan. "Peer Interaction in the First Year of Life: An Examination

of Structure, Content, and Sensitivity to Toys."
Child Development (1980): 51, 481-488.

Vygotsky, L. S. *Thought and Language*. Cambridge: MIT
Press, 1962.